LaserMonks

LaserMonks

The Business Story nine Hundred Years in the Making

SARAH CANIGLIA

AND

CINDY GRIFFITH

New York   Chicago   San Francisco   Lisbon
London   Madrid   Mexico City   Milan   New Delhi
San Juan   Seoul   Singapore   Sydney   Toronto

1 2 3 4 5 6 7 8 9 0   DOC/DOC 0 9 8 7

ISBN-13: 978-0-07-149571-4
ISBN-10:   0-07-149571-1

McGraw-Hill books are available at special quantity discounts to use
as premiums and sales promotions, or for use in corporate training
programs. For more information, please write to the Director of
Special Sales, Professional Publishing, McGraw-Hill, Two Penn Plaza,
New York, NY 10121-2298. Or contact your local bookstore.

Library of Congress Cataloging-in-Publication Data

Caniglia, Sarah.
  LaserMonks / by Sarah Caniglia and Cindy Griffith.
    p. cm.
  ISBN-13: 978-0-07-149571-4
  ISBN-10: 0-07-149571-1
  1. LaserMonks (Firm) 2. Printing ink industry--United States. 3.
Toners (Xerography) industry--United States. 4. Office equipment and
supplies industry--United States. I. Griffith, Cindy. II. Title.
III.
Title: Laser monks.
HD9792.U54L373 2008
381'.4568160973--dc22
                                                          2007032955
This book is printed on acid-free paper.

*This book is dedicated to our fathers,
who instilled in us both the entrepreneurial
spirit and the strong work ethic needed
to be successful in our endeavors.*

contents

acknowledgments

Many thanks and blessings to all of the monks of Our Lady of Spring Bank Cistercian Abbey, without whom this book would never have been written. Their generosity and benevolence helps needy people in many communities and their prayer gives comfort to the world.

In particular, we are forever grateful to Father Bernard McCoy and Father Robert Keffer, who hold their monastic community together with grace and love and have taught us the true balance of St. Benedict's teachings.

Warm blessings to the Ludick family who have shown us, through their daily actions and their spirit, the meaning of Christian charity.

There are several key people in our MonkHelper Marketing and LaserMonks family that need mention: Thank you to Victoria, our friend and peer, who is the glue that holds the office together; thank you and cheers to Chris for working with us through times of chaos and deadlines; gratitude to Melissa, who manages to know the answer to every question asked of her and to her husband, Tim, for all his early morning trips; and many thanks to the ladies at the Greenery, who always provide us with good conversation and keep us apprised of town happenings.

Thank you to our many loyal customers, who support our good works through their purchases and who remain the cornerstone of our business.

Thank you to our mothers, who raised us with strength and determination, and who support us unconditionally.

From Cindy:

Love to Jim and Sherryl, the brother and sister who playfully tormented me as a child, and whom I idolize to this day. To Carol and Tony for putting up with my siblings, and to all of the intelligent, hilarious, and loving nieces and nephews who resulted from the above unions.

To my children and best friends, Erica and Michael, who have filled me with pride every day for the last 22 years. To my granddaughters Audra and Alayna, who legitimize my reason for being.

From Sarah:

Love and respect to all those family members, living and deceased, for the profound impact on my life and who instilled in me the idea that humor and determination go a long way toward being a success.

This project would not have come about without the nurturing of Melissa Bonventre, who was our biggest champion, nor without the guidance of Jeanne Glasser, our editor at McGraw-Hill.

A special thanks to Marcia Layton-Turner, who collaborated with us with professionalism and grace through this process as first-time authors.

Last, but most certainly not least, we would like to thank Rudy, Snowball, Bailey, Snickerdoodle, Peach, Gus, and all of the other canines—past and present—who have provided us with companionship every day. They are always here with a ready smile and a wagging tail, no matter how busy we are, no matter how late we are in the office working. They teach us compassion and unconditional love every day, and without them, we would be lost.

LaserMonks

introduction

How did five Cistercian monks from Wisconsin create a multimillion dollar Internet ink and toner business that now sustains their order and their local community? That's the tale told in this book. What originated as a means of sustaining a single abbey has evolved into a role model that other businesses are clamoring to follow.

The story is surprising for a number of reasons, not the least of which is that monks and the business world don't often work hand-in-hand. The priorities of an abbey, of a monastic order, are rarely in harmony with capitalism and business pursuits, mainly because monks commit themselves to a life of prayer, not profit.

▦ Being Called

It is not a simple thing, becoming a monk. Men who feel this "calling" have usually spent a great deal of time assessing their lives, contemplating their place in this world. Realizing this "calling" is merely the first step on a road to finding their inner balance. They have made their decision, but then what?

Leaving their home, their careers, their families, their bank accounts, and everything they own, they begin their journey to find a contemplative community that best fits their personality, and where all agree that they will fill a missing piece of the monastic puzzle. Arriving on the steps of a monastery, these novices have severed ties with all that is familiar, all that is comfortable. They have given up all their property, all their assets, and vowed that from this point in their lives, everything revolves around God and "community." Home is the monastery, a sparsely furnished "cell," meals eaten together as a community, and many hours of daily prayer. Monks pray at times when most laypeople, the people these novices used to be, are sleeping, and even still when laypeople are rushing to and from jobs in the secular world. Getting used to a slow-paced, ordered life of prayer and peaceful contemplation is never easy, even for those who know in their hearts that this is where they belong.

In addition to prayer, Cistercian monks are also expected to contribute to their abbey's self-sufficiency. Cistercian monasteries have always been self-supporting, that is they do not rely on donations but on funds they have earned through work of their own hands. They assess the time, talents, and treasures of each member of the community to determine what sort of business venture might be most able to support the abbey. Does one of the monks have culinary skills? Baking bread or canning jams and jellies might make for a successful venture. Is there a carpenter in the group? Perhaps selling wood carvings, or building caskets might work. These fairly straightforward, simple types of businesses are what have sustained many of the monastic communities that have tried them.

A Business Idea Emerges

Flash-forward to 2001, and to a very small order of Cistercian monks in Sparta, Wisconsin. Our Lady of Spring Bank Cistercian Abbey was struggling to find a solid means of supporting its community. Many ideas had crossed the minds of the five monks, and some ventures were attempted. When Father Bernard found that the toner for his laser printer needed replacing, the seed of what would become LaserMonks.com was planted. He realized that if his community was struggling with the high cost of these necessary everyday office items, so too were other religious communities, schools, and nonprofit organizations. It dawned on him that if he could find a way to save money on these items, he could pass the savings on to other organizations in similar need.

By 2007, this seed of an idea had become what is arguably one of the most complex business models run by a monastery. Ink and toner is a huge industry.

There are thousands of machines on the market, and thousands upon thousands of ink and toner products to fit these machines. The natural outgrowth from ink and toner products is office supplies—all the same items that the major office supply chains sell. With these products, in addition to various goods made by other monasteries, and Benevolent Blends Coffee, LaserMonks' online database now boasts more than 35,000 different products, and a high-tech online business to handle the 300–500 orders per day. With this diversity of offerings, it was natural for Laser-Monks to launch a network of Web microsites to better showcase individual product lines, and efficiently handle the increased interest our customers have shown.

But what of the monks? What of the peaceful serenity of monastic prayer and charity? This is the most difficult line for monastic groups to straddle. How do we sustain our abbey, and our charitable outreach, and still maintain our ordered life of monastic prayer and solemnity?

Through the ages, monastic communities have relied on laypeople to assist in running their business endeavors. When we came to Wisconsin in July of 2003, we offered our services free of charge to help launch the monk's online business. The monks, as they have through history, offered us—their modern-day laypeople—room, board, and whatever we needed to be comfortable while we were there. Over time our involvement and responsibility for the monks' business has expanded to the point that we now successfully manage every aspect of the Laser-Monks business through our company, MonkHelper Marketing, Inc. Although we are not monks or nuns, MonkHelper Marketing, Inc., has somehow filled another piece of Our Lady of Spring Banks Cistercian Abbey's monastic puzzle. We are the piece that allows them to continue their life of prayer and good works.

Today, LaserMonks is frequently cited by other companies as an example of how to incorporate charity into a business model. The concept of socially conscious purchasing is not new, but the application of monastic teachings and principles to a for-profit venture is. Social entrepreneurism is also not new, but LaserMonks' policy of distributing profits across needy communities, organizations, and individuals is, and gives us a competitive advantage that further fuels the company's growth. Customers prefer to buy from us because they know they are purchasing a quality product, with a side benefit of supporting the needy worldwide. And other businesses are starting to take note.

Companies as far away as the United Kingdom have used our Customer Care as an example of how to efficiently run a business. This book will explore how we started, how we have grown, and all we have learned along the way. By the time this is published, we will surely have learned more lessons about business and charity. Our hope is now that we have plowed the furrow, and planted the seed, your company and many charitable causes can benefit from our harvest.

chapter
one

A Leap
of Faith

W E DIDN'T REALIZE IT AT THE TIME, BUT OUR LIVES WERE FOREVER CHANGED THE MOMENT WE DROVE, WITH SOME HESITANCE, THROUGH THE GATES OF THE ABBEY OF OUR LADY OF SPRING BANK IN JULY 2003. OUR JOURNEY HAD BEEN A LONG ONE, AS WE HAD DRIVEN SEVERAL THOUSAND MILES ACROSS COUNTRY. WHEN WE ARRIVED WE WERE WEARY, THIRSTY, AND ENTIRELY UNSURE OF WHAT TO EXPECT.

As we drove up the dirt-and-gravel road to the monastery, we were greeted by our hosts, the six monks who had devoted their lives and souls to God, the abbey, and each other. That they all came out to warmly greet us with their 900-year-old tradition of "Cistercian Hospitality" surprised us, but it shouldn't have. Over time we have tried to weave that practice of hospitality, of welcoming and care, into our service of LaserMonks' customers.

Included in our greeting party that day were a Doberman Pinscher named Ludwig (a gentle and docile Dobie who sits and lies down to commands in Latin), and an Egyptian Pharaoh Hound named Luxor. Oh, and the duck. One of the junior monks had adopted a baby duck and had taken on its care as part of his daily routine. We watched, as did these monks in heavy muslin robes with black hooded scapulars, as the duckling waded in a small pool set up behind the monastery.

At the time our thoughts were twofold: It was in the upper 90's with 100 percent humidity and these men never complained, nor did they really seem to notice the heat or the Japanese beetles that were pestering us all. It struck us that taking care of people and things seemed to be second nature to these monks.

Although the monks were true to their calling and very hospitable, we were both annoyed by the weather, the bugs, and lack of sleep. Anxious to see if our journey was ending or just beginning, we were beckoned through the doors of the abbey to share lunch, which always begins and ends with prayer.

Walking over that threshold, we felt as if we had taken a giant step from the 21st century back a few thousand years.

We were out of our element and, at first, did not speak at all because we just assumed the monks ate in silence. We soon learned that they frequently do observe silence at meals, but not when dining with guests. We also learned that these men were educated, spoke a multitude of languages, and were very well traveled. The adventure was becoming much more interesting!

During our lunch, a feast prepared by Father Robert, a chef among monks, we learned about the lifestyle in a monastic holy order. Cistercian monks, though Catholic, are distanced from the "real world" of organized religion—some call them loners—because they pray for the world on their own terms. We learned of their observance of prayer at regimented times during the day and that they follow the Rule of St. Benedict, a sort of "monastic guideline" for living. The monks walk in silence after Compline at 7:00 p.m. and remain silent until Vigils at 4:45 a.m., we learned, with six scheduled times of prayer between Vigils and Compline. We heard about the cloistered areas within the walls of the monastery, and on the grounds. We saw the prayer book at the entrance to the chapel, with letters containing prayer requests from across the country—prayers that are taken very seriously and never overlooked.

What dawned on us both, after learning just this small amount about monastic life, was that we wanted to be a part of this. We felt a personal need to support these benevolent men so that they could continue to follow their calling without having to worry about how their business was performing. In many ways, this was possibly the beginning of our "calling."

What we didn't know at the time was that the monks were at a crossroads. Their cheerfulness and warmth at meeting us belied the fact that they were struggling to find a successful way to support the abbey. In fact, this abbey was no different than other abbeys in their need for successful ventures.

In an effort to find a way of making the monastery self-sustaining, the monks of Our Lady of Spring Bank had tried many avenues to generate income. At one time or another, they had considered everything from growing shiitake mushrooms to relocating houses to opening a world-class golf course. Unfortunately, these ideas did not come to fruition. The monks had spent a great deal of their time, talent, and resources in unsuccessful bids to get these ventures off the ground. Fortunately, the Cistercians have a history of turning possible defeat into ultimate success.

After lunch, Father Bernard McCoy (who is now Prior of the abbey) drove with us to the abbey's retreat house, called the Hermitage, which was 90 minutes away from the abbey itself. Six hundred feet above the Mississippi River, where you can feast on spectacular views in three states—Wisconsin, Iowa, and Minnesota—the Hermitage is a sort of retreat for the spiritually searching. Frequently used for dignitaries and visiting friends, and for weekend retreats for the monks themselves, the facility is a three-bedroom home up in the hills, far away from civilization, or so it seemed, equipped with all the comforts of home in addition to a peaceful chapel on the lower level.

We had been invited to take advantage of the Hermitage's offerings, and the monk's hospitality, at the behest of Father Bernard, based on a single phone call.

Entrepreneurs in our own right, we had initially been intrigued by the monks' business model and had contacted the monks just out of curiosity (always keeping in the back of our minds that there could be an opportunity here).

▦ The "Angels" Arrive

Father Bernard's need for replacement ink for his printer one day, and his astonishment at the huge mark-up companies were charging on such cartridges, spawned an idea that took hold. A brilliant man with big ideas, Father Bernard envisioned providing a less expensive source for ink and toner that could generate a modest income for the abbey. After having spent time, energy, and money on other ventures, this one would have to start small, he knew, but he also saw great potential. The other monks supported the idea and they began researching the industry. Their first notion was to collect and remanufacture toner cartridges on the abbey grounds. With so few monks to do the labor-intensive work, and to keep up with increase in demand, Father Bernard soon realized that there was a more efficient way to reach more customers: drop-shipping from established remanufacturers.

At its start in 2002, LaserMonks.com consisted of a few monks filling two or three orders a day, with sales of $2,500 the first year. With the uniqueness of the business and after a few media mentions, the number of daily orders climbed to between ten and twenty. Unfortunately, that was barely enough to keep the electricity on or the cupboards filled with food. Their start-up was struggling, and they knew there had to be some way to kick-start the business.

Initially, the business started without much fanfare. After all, they started the company with only a few thousand dollars in capital and no knowledge of the ink and toner business. Realistically, how well could they do?, the skeptics asked.

What these skeptics did not understand was that the monks had going for them a 1,500-year tradition of creative survivalism and the drive—no, the necessity—to be self-sustaining.

▥ Against the Odds

Google the words "inkjet cartridge" or "toner cartridge" and you'll be overwhelmed by the number of online retailers offering such products. The millions of listings you'll see reflect the tens of thousands of ink and toner sites currently on the Internet. While their total numbers have grown in the last decade, the names have changed many times. Just as the majority of start-ups fail, so do ink and toner sites. Many have come and gone just as quickly, after discovering how difficult it is to grab market share from existing sites and leverage it.

The ink and toner industry is highly competitive with ever-shrinking margins—hardly a business any management consultant would recommend starting. And yet the monks were already in it when we discovered them. But they were struggling.

So when the monks received a call from two inquisitive businesswomen about their venture, they sensed there might be an opportunity for mutual benefit. They bade us come to the Midwest to, as they put it, "relax and discover Wisconsin." At the time, the two of us were successful entrepreneurs in assisting businesses in their e-commerce efforts. Our backgrounds were very diverse—from Internet marketing and Web site design to years in the medical industry, we were the ultimate multitaskers by raising families at the same time. Any challenge we took on, whether it be starting a new company or raising children, had always been successful.

▦ Unlikely Stewards

We did relax for a couple of days, enjoying the peacefulness of the Hermitage, until we recognized the monks' need for help. They needed marketing guidance, graphic design support, production help, even someone to take customer service calls during the seven to eight times a day that they prayed. So we offered our services to give their business a push in the right direction—

between us we had years of experience in marketing and technology. In return, they offered accommodations and all the support the monks could provide. We were curious about them and they were probably equally curious about us: could these two women figure out how to increase the momentum of this business venture?

Our aim has always been to let the monks be monks, focusing on their life of prayer, while we built the business. With a quality product, low cost, and talented marketers, we were sure it would be fairly straightforward. Of course, we were wrong. It wasn't that simple.

We quickly discovered that although the idea of monks owning a business using twenty-first century technology was a novel one, it was not a unique enough selling proposition to sustain the business. We had a business concept and monks, that was all. We lacked capital, employees, funds for marketing, and support from the local business community. Even after many months of volunteering our services in support of the abbey, we seemed to be no further along in helping them make it a viable business.

Then one evening, as we watched the sun set over the cornfields surrounding the monastery, a new business strategy emerged that would change LaserMonks forever.

Commerce with Compassion

As we watched the sun slip behind the hills, and the room became dim, we reflected on personal experiences we have had as consumers. We gradually realized that what could make this business unique and successful was our ability to infuse it with that same personal care that monks have historically provided. Monasteries were founded on the principle of hospitality, with a commitment to providing shelter for weary travelers. It didn't matter if the abbey could barely feed its own community, any traveler was welcome and was treated as a truly special guest. Likewise, abbeys have traditionally initiated and supported good works in the communities surrounding them, providing needed assistance.

Having been at the abbey for months now, we had begun to hear of the quiet help the monks of Our Lady of Spring Bank routinely provide to their community. The Cistercians have a tradition of putting others' needs first, helping members of the community even when they have so little to spare. They give scholarships and provide financial support to families in need. They quietly, and anonymously, step in to intervene when they see the opportunity.

We saw their generosity firsthand with one of our *monkhelpers*, the term we gave those of us who were pitching in to assist the abbey. This particular monkhelper is now the cornerstone of the Laser-Monks' customer service department, handling much of the customer issues or questions that come up. She is a tremendous worker and a huge asset to Laser-Monks. She is also a single mom raising three children on her own, and when she needed financial help in moving to a better place to live, the monks offered their assistance, never asking for repayment and never expecting it. Despite the fact that the business was struggling, the monks' instincts were to help others.

What if we could combine a for-profit venture with that same sense of civic responsibility that is at the core of the monks' lifestyle? A combination of capitalism and social entrepreneurism could differentiate LaserMonks from the many other discount ink and toner e-tailers out there.

Faced with the option of purchasing the same product from two different companies—one of which donated the bulk of its proceeds to charity—we knew in our hearts that consumers would give the business to the company that was more than a profit center. And that became our unique selling proposition, offering consumers the opportunity to purchase lower cost products *and* support good works. All things being equal, who wouldn't want to help support needy people and organizations, we said to ourselves. It could be a win-win proposition and blessing for all.

From that point on, our bottom line was not profit, but charitable works. To this day, the more money LaserMonks makes, the more money is available to donate to needy organizations.

We also altered our marketing strategy. We went from focusing on ink and toner sold by monks to selling ink and toner that can *change lives*. Our goal was to change the purchasing patterns of consumers, giving them the opportunity to choose to make a purchase with a purpose, a purchase that would support worthy charitable organizations and not-for-profits worldwide.

Step-by-step, we wove social entrepreneurism and participation into our daily operations.

It worked. With the help of its customers, LaserMonks became much more than a unique source of ink and toner, it became a sustainable venture that made a difference. LaserMonks' sales doubled in 2003, 2004, and 2005 as the message of buying with a purpose resonated with consumers. As sales soared, so did customer retention, helping to keep our marketing and operational costs down. Without a brick-and-mortar operation, we manage to run a streamlined business with very little overhead. We employ the latest technology in order to deliver a quality product and speedy delivery, which gives customers competitive rates while still keeping our profit margins higher than the industry average. But we also do just about everything ourselves.

While the monks spend their days praying, ministering, tending to their 600 acres and living lives of contemplation, we run LaserMonks. We handle the entire business from top to bottom, from all the upper management and corporate duties to the daily operations, marketing, media, relations and everything in between. Over the last few years, we have enlisted the assistance of monkhelpers for the day-to-day business, while we concentrate on management, media and marketing, charity, and new product branding.

Even when the business reached multimillion-dollar status, its operations didn't change. We decided that as the business became more successful we would keep the operation's core business model and the grass roots feel. With our growth, we also came to the realization that we had other talents. With our mission of using profit to help others, we knew that any money spent for outside services would be money taken from the hands of the needy. We opted not to enlist consultants to advise us on branding, changing the company's image, or marketing strategy because our in-house marketing is what had made us successful. And so, with the talents and treasures of the monks along with MonkHelper Marketing, Inc., LaserMonks is lean, focused, and as streamlined a business as you will encounter. We would rather give back to the communities and families worldwide that need it than spend profits needlessly.

In small ways, we started to shift the perception of what a business stands for in the community. Instead of a greedy monster whose sole purpose is profit, we demonstrated to customers that this venture cares as much about the needy as we do about our bottom line. In a nutshell, we created a win-win proposition that benefits our customers, the monks, and the community at large.

Now we want to help other businesses change the way they operate, too.

▦ Faith and Hard Work

By sharing with you how we approached the success of LaserMonks, and how we managed to carve out a profitable niche within a very low-margin, highly competitive industry, we hope that you will be inspired to find a way to use your extra profits to do good works in *your* community.

In this chapter you heard all about how we became part of LaserMonks, how we repositioned the company, and how we knew we were on the right track. Chapter Two tells you how we carved out a niche with social entrepreneurism as the unique selling proposition (USP). Chapter Three describes the Rule of St. Benedict and how it guides the lives of the monks and the way in which LaserMonks does business. We'll also offer examples and guidelines on how you can incorporate the Rule into your own business. Chapters Four and Five are about how we became a socially conscious business and embedded charitable works into our daily operations. After telling you about how we did that, we explain how any company can use social entrepreneurship as a marketing tool. And Chapter Six is about developing a successful e-commerce business. Even after crafting our USP and marketing strategy, the business model still could have failed had we not put into place a basic technology infrastructure to support it. We'll tell you about the key players in a successful e-commerce business and how to coordinate them for success. Along the way you'll also learn about the history of, and life within, the Cistercian order, their tradition of entrepreneurship, and the common practice of hiring lay people to manage their business endeavors.

While LaserMonks is certainly unique, many of our business principles and practices are tried and true. If you apply our business model and marketing tactics you, too, may see both your profits and your philanthropy rise. That is our hope for you.

chapter
two

the
Lasermonks
story

"O YOU TWO KNOW ANYTHING ABOUT MICROSOFT EXCEL?" FATHER BERNARD ASKED US ONE MORNING. ONE OF THE MOST DAUNTING CHALLENGES FOR A MONK, OR ANYONE COMMITTED TO MONASTIC LIFE, IS FINDING THE BALANCE BETWEEN WORK AND PRAYER. WITH THIS SIMPLE INQUIRY, FATHER BERNARD HAD STARTED ON THE COURSE TO BALANCING HIS OWN MONASTIC LIFE, AND THAT OF ALL THE MONKS OF OUR LADY of Spring Bank Cistercian Abbey. Cistercian monastic communities are called to a life of prayer and charity, but once committed to this life, they have the added responsibility of being self-supporting. These two responsibilities are equally important, and there is a daily struggle to address each individually without the other suffering.

After spending a few days in his presence, enjoying the monks' hospitality and observing the LaserMonks operation, we knew Father Bernard was extremely bright and observant. He didn't usually ask a question unless he was fairly sure he knew the answer.

"Sure, what do you need?" we replied, since Excel is one of the many software programs in which we are well-versed.

He handed us a stack of papers listing at least two thousand ink and toner cartridges. Next to each cartridge name and product code was a column designating the corresponding printers that used that particular ink. This column was conspicuously bare. Not every ink and toner listing was complete. There were key pieces of information missing on each piece of paper.

"Do you think you can help us finish this?," Father Bernard asked. "This is our start of an ink and toner database. With our schedule of prayer, it would take us forever to complete. We monks are slow beasts. It would help us tremendously if you could complete the project." He was taking a chance, really, asking for help from two outsiders—businesswomen who had only recently arrived at the abbey. Again, we sensed he already knew the answer.

Of course, what he really meant was, "Can you help us get this fledgling e-commerce business off the ground?" Because that was what he needed. Fortunately, that was exactly what the finished Excel database could do: give customers the information they need to order online. Customers would be able to enter their particular printer's make and model and the LaserMonks Web site could tell them which replacement ink or toner was a match. A few buttons later and the product was ordered, paid for, and waiting to be shipped by LaserMonks.

That was Father Bernard's vision for LaserMonks, but there was quite a bit of work required to make it a reality. Apparently, we were there to do just that: Make it a reality.

"So What Else Can You Do?"

For the next few months both of us, and occasionally Father Bernard, sat in his office in the basement of the abbey, which was only slightly bigger than a walk-in closet, and worked at creating a full catalog of ink and toner. That meant researching compatible and genuine ink and toner for inkjet and laser printers, copiers, and fax machines.

We were much more than typists, however. Before even starting this task, we developed a systematic plan for giving the monks what they needed. Instead of jumping right in and making the changes we felt were necessary for the business to be successful, we examined what they had, analyzed what was missing, and then developed a list of tasks we needed to complete in order to help the monks achieve their mission.

In addition to repaying the monks for their generous hospitality by doing this work, we also wanted to show them how we approach tasks. Although they never said it, we felt we were interviewing for a job of sorts: the opportunity to become more involved in the management of the LaserMonks' business. But first we had to prove to the monks we were what they needed.

After several weeks of this tedious but critical work, Father Bernard saw that we worked tirelessly, but that we could use a new challenge. He was right. Sitting glued to the computer for hours on end, typing database entries, was becoming mind-numbing. Fortunately, we were nearly done.

"So what else can you do?" Father Bernard asked one morning in August. Again, he knew the answer. "Maybe you could help us with the Web site design?" he suggested.

Now, the original Web site the monks had developed was certainly functional. It had a basic shopping cart that allowed customers to search for the ink or toner they needed, and to pay using one of four payment types. But the server was down intermittently and we discovered that the merchant processor was not known for issuing payments in a timely manner.

We began to make changes, little-by-little, page-by-page to the Web site. We saw that the monks needed our assistance, and the more we learned about them and their business, the more we wanted to be part of their venture. But we didn't want to overstep any bounds. We worked hard at balancing our assertive personalities with patience, taking it slowly and building the confidence and trust of the monks every step of the way.

At the time, we were working out of Father Bernard's office and from the Hermitage, where there was a dial-up computer available. Yes, dial-up. We eventually moved from the Hermitage into another abbey-owned property closer to the monastery, where broadband Internet service was available. We continued to work as volunteers, not knowing where this effort might lead, but happy for the opportunity to be of service.

By fall, Father Bernard was comfortable enough with us that he decided we could handle the incoming e-mail messages and order processing. To the monks, the five to ten orders a day was overwhelming, even with the help of a high school student who had been answering phones and e-mails on their behalf. So we were permitted to assume that responsibility, but the phones were still off-limits.

We had many ideas for what the Web site could do and look like, but money was not readily available for most of our brilliant ideas. So we did what we could without funds, continuing to slowly revamp the site and inject some personality and much needed content, which we felt it lacked.

In October, Father Bernard had another question for us: "Why don't you stay? We can't pay you now, but we can give you a place to stay," he offered.

Having invested so much of ourselves already in helping to shape what LaserMonks could be we weren't ready to walk away, despite the lack of a salary. "Why don't we stay two months and see how it goes," we proposed. Two months later, we moved onto the abbey property and began work on a plan for growing Laser-Monks to the point where it could afford to pay us for our work. That's what was needed—more revenue, more customers—and it was up to us to generate both.

▣ Planning for Success

Once we decided to formally stay and help run Laser-Monks, we began crafting a more comprehensive business plan—something that hadn't yet been done for the enterprise.

We started by making a list of the things the business already had, its tangible and intangible assets. These included the corporate name, the corresponding Web site URL, a product line for sale, e-commerce capabilities on the Web site, merchant account status for credit card acceptance, an ink and toner vendor, and a general idea of why customers were buying from the company.

We also examined the four key business drivers: initial consumer shopping experience, product quality, customer service, and pricing.

Shopping Experience

As a purely online business without a brick-and-mortar retail component, LaserMonks attains customers via the Internet, at the company's Web site. The customer's first impression is shaped almost entirely by the look and feel of the site. Understanding this, we placed a priority on reshaping the existing Web site to better match LaserMonks' mission and identity.

The original Web site, designed by Father Bernard, was very basic, mainly out of necessity. Father Bernard had some limited business and computer programming knowledge and he was able to put together a site that made purchases of ink and toner cartridges possible. We were impressed by what he had accomplished. We also saw the opportunity to make some changes that might encourage customers to establish a long-term buying relationship with LaserMonks.

So we started by breaking the entire Web site apart and then gradually putting it back together. We wanted the site to be more user-friendly and inspirational for visitors.

We first added information about the company and why and how the profits go to support good works worldwide. We felt that was a key reason that customers might buy from us instead of from a major office products chain or from ultracheap competitors. The site began evolving, and is still evolving, to try to meet the needs and preferences of our customer base, as well as to keep pace with Web site technology.

We were aware that our customers wanted a site that was more advanced technologically, with more information about new products and charitable giving content, because we asked them. We regularly poll and survey our customers to find out what they want to learn from the site and which changes or revisions they would like to see in the business. And then, with our limited budget, we try to accommodate them. We recognized the importance of customer feedback early on. And not just feedback about quality of product, or pricing, but about their complete LaserMonks Web site experience.

Simple things, such as the size or color of the font used, are important factors in whether a customer has a good Web experience or a miserable one. We listen to each comment, and make every effort to change in response to customers' needs.

Product Quality

Father Bernard's initial vision was to provide ink and toner at lower prices to schools, nonprofit groups, and religious organizations. He chose this particular market because of the monks' commitment to helping those in need. Like the monastery, these groups, and others with limited—almost nonexistent—budgets, could benefit from a lower cost source for expensive ink and toner cartridges.

His focus was on a lower cost product, but we decided early on that the quality of the product trumped pricing. We researched our product cost, did an in-depth study of what the market will bear price-wise online, talked to customers, and set some parameters regarding how much we wanted to be able to donate.

We believed that as long as we had a quality product we could build solid customer relationships on which the company would grow. Conversely, if we tried to be the lowest cost provider of ink and toner to nonprofit groups and budget-conscious organizations, we would probably drive ourselves out of business through escalating price wars with online competitors.

Customer Service

Another way we believed we could differentiate Laser-Monks, and build a core following, was through the quality of our customer service. But we aimed to do more than just serve customers, we wanted to astound them.

Fortunately, we were backed by 900 years of Cistercian history. As we have said, the Cistercian order is known for its emphasis on hospitality, on providing whatever guests of the abbey require, perhaps even before they realized they need it. The importance of hospitality and service to visitors and guests is a natural outcome of the Rule of St. Benedict, which guides the monks' life. One of the chapters of *The Rule of St. Benedict* reads:

> *"Let all guests that come be received like Christ Himself, for He will say, 'I was a stranger and ye took Me in.' And let fitting honour be shown to all, especially such as are of the household of the faith and to wayfarers . . ."*

The Rule goes on to specify exactly how strangers should be treated, with a special personal greeting on arrival at the abbey, with bowing and prostration, with cleansing of the feet. Monastery construction was even guided by the importance of showing special courtesy to guests, such as the call for separate guest kitchens, so that they might have ease of access at any hour of the day or night. They even went so far as to construct special buildings for their visitors to enjoy. However, if the traveler's stay exceeded a week, he or she was expected to return the favor in the form of work for the monastery.

Understanding that we were the equivalent of those long-ago travelers, we worked to return the monks' hospitality, and to introduce it to our customers. Our two call-center workers also supported that effort, by answering customer calls and doing what was necessary to make them feel special.

Pricing

Although LaserMonks was originally positioned as a low-cost provider, our own research indicated there was no more competition at the middle or high end of the market than at the low end. We decided we might as well move upmarket and generate more revenue with which to sustain the monastery. But there was also a lot of trial and error along the way.

For example, even as the business began to grow, we thought that "price-matching" might help Laser-Monks gain a corporate clientele. We quickly learned that this was not a smart strategy for us. The customers who were attracted to such an offer were always more concerned about price than loyalty, while we were more concerned about loyalty than price. This wasn't a way to establish a strong customer base. It wasn't a good fit.

Now our strategy is to have the best quality product with reasonably competitive pricing, in the belief that when faced with similar products of similar price, customers will purchase from the company that uses the proceeds for good works. That's our position, which resonates with consumers, both current and potential.

Fortunately, Cone, Inc. backs us up. In their recent survey of consumers they learned that 80 percent of consumers say that, all things being equal, they are more likely to spend their dollars on companies that support charitable causes. In addition, Cone found that 92 percent of Americans think it is important for companies to make charitable contributions, or to donate products and/or services to nonprofit organizations in their community. Despite this clear consumer preference for socially responsible businesses, LaserMonks is still a rarity.

▦ Mission: Profitability

Over the next few months we worked on giving LaserMonks a personality that was attractive to customers. We also made another list, this time of all the areas we needed to address and then a summary of where we were at the moment with respect to each line item. We also created three-month, six-month, and nine-month milestones for each area to help us gauge our progress down the line.

And despite the fact that we had very little money coming in at the start, we prepared sales and expense projections. We needed more profits to support the monks, to support all the charitable works we wanted to do, and to enable the business to pay us. That would take a major growth spurt. But we were up to the challenge. That's one thing about the two of us; when we accept a challenge, we face it head on with optimism and determination. LaserMonks was no different. We were determined to be successful.

We started by expanding our inventory. What began as a few hundred items grew to several thousand in just a few months. This was our first priority because we had seen consumers come to the site and then leave when they could not find the ink or toner cartridge they needed. They couldn't find it because we didn't carry it. So we worked on carrying a broader selection to meet customer needs.

We spent a lot of time researching all the printers, copiers, and fax machines currently on the market, and then updating the site with products and descriptions of ink and toner cartridges that fit those models. And yes, this meant we were back to the old Excel spreadsheet that started this whole venture.

Then we began to evaluate vendors. We had one vendor that drop-shipped orders, which was so much simpler than stocking inventory and mailing orders out from Our Lady of Spring Bank. What we needed at this point, were more drop ship–capable vendors.

With a list of half-dozen or so companies, we examined each potential supplier from a variety of perspectives: their wholesale price, their reputation for quality, number of drop ship warehouses, delivery accuracy and, most importantly, their understanding of and support for our ultimate mission. We needed vendors that "got" us and understood our mission.

Unfortunately, because we were so small, few vendors were even willing to negotiate their prices. Our mission of charitable giving, and why we were different, mattered less to them than the fact that they considered LaserMonks "small potatoes." They just weren't interested in doing business with us. But that didn't stop us from pushing and prodding them to take a look at our business model. We didn't accept "no" the first time or the tenth time or the hundredth time, we just kept asking them for better pricing and to consider developing a long-term relationship with us. And we tried to help them see how large Laser-Monks was going to grow.

▓ Lack of Revenue Necessitates Creativity

Of course, every entrepreneur has big plans for his or her business at the outset, and few ever achieve their lofty goals. But we were committed to this venture, to helping the monks, and we knew we would succeed. Flash forward four years and we have vendors who claim to "get us," and what our mission means to those less fortunate. We also have vendor wannabes who would stand on their heads to call us a client.

Just this morning we had a well-known manu-facturer of color toner call us for the hundredth time.

This sales rep has been calling several times a month, asking us to carry their product. She went so far as to send us product samples and a brand new printer in which to use them, in an effort to win our business back. Years ago we *had* carried their brand, but stopped when our printer malfunctioned while using their products. Since then, they have been trying to woo us back.

We are still a very small dealer comparatively speaking, and were somewhat surprised by the lengths she was going to, in an effort to get us back as a dealer. We asked her why it was so important to win back our business.

She told us, "We're focused on LaserMonks because of who you are and what you stand for. Gaining your business is very important to our company." In addition, she wanted us to be the lead dealer marketing their products. What a shift from just a few years ago when we struggled to convince vendors to work with us! It was so gratifying to hear a vendor tell us that *our* business was important to *them*.

There were several vendors, however, who were willing to work with us in the early days and are the same vendors we use today. As we said, loyalty is important and we are loyal to our suppliers as they have been loyal to us.

Despite the lean times, we were determined to prepare the business for its ultimate success. We crafted manuals on customer care and hospitality to guide our current and future employees, and wrote scripts for incoming phone calls, all to ensure that customers were being given the greatest care and attention. We wanted to be sure that callers would receive the same level of attention when LaserMonks became a multimillion dollar business as they did now, with three people manning the phones.

We also began working on the Web site in earnest, adding content and transforming its personality to better reflect LaserMonks' overall mission: helping others.

To give the site a more charitable feel, we added content reflecting our good works projects. People could then read about what we were doing and be reassured that we actually did what we said we would. In that way, we also built trust with potential and current customers. We also added things to the home page, such as "the charity of the month." This was designed to show visitors at least one of the charities we were donating to during that particular month.

We reminded site visitors we were a different kind of company, reinforcing that message on pages we knew they would visit, such as ink and toner category pages and the checkout page. Our look became less like competitive ink and toner sites, and more about charity and good works. We don't splatter product images across our home page because we feel customers will find their items through our menu. What makes us different is what we do *after* the purchase. This is what we wanted to convey to the consumer.

When new products were added to the site, including products from other monasteries, we reminded customers that the proceeds went to charity, and reminded them again within the product descriptions. We also added books and music, then batteries and data storage media. Most recently, we rolled out LaserMonks-branded caps and T-shirts, and a new line of coffee specially blended and roasted for us, appropriately named "Benevolent Blends." We also have plans to introduce a multitude of additional products including several blends of olive oil and a printer service plan.

We did something similar with our recycling program. Each order placed with LaserMonks is accompanied by a self-addressed plastic bag for collecting used ink cartridges, which we recycle. At the Web site, we let customers know that when they recycle their cartridges with us, all *that* money goes to charity, too. Not only are they helping the environment, but they're donating yet again to a worthy cause.

We created a tag line to more clearly communicate what makes us different. What began as "Real Savings. Real Monks. Supporting real people" morphed to "Saving you money. Serving those in need." And it is evolving again as we write, to "Commerce with Compassion."

Along with our marketing message, we incorporated some marketing programs, such as the "Random Acts of Kindness" campaign. We let site visitors know that if they sent us a written story about an act of kindness they performed, or an act of kindness which touched their life in some way, they would receive a discount on their next order. We want to reward customers for any part they can play in doing good works within their own community. That's part of our mission, too. And it doesn't cost much to do.

As we were shifting the Web site's emphasis, from low-cost ink and toner to ink and toner sales yielding charitable works, we were also shifting consumer perception of LaserMonks in the marketplace. Father Bernard's idea was to be the David to the national chain's Goliath, using compatible products to keep costs low for customers. Initially we did not sell genuine brand name products from companies like HP, Canon, and Lexmark because they were higher cost than the compatible alternatives. Remember, we started out to save schools, churches, and nonprofit groups money, by offering low-cost alternative products. But our customers wanted the option to buy brand name products and we learned that it simply makes sense to offer what customers need, so we eventually began selling both.

Our research also made it clear to us that compatible or remanufactured ink and toner had a negative perception. LaserMonks' image was affected by association. Sure, many businesses, schools, and nonprofit organizations insisted on purchasing brand name products, but we didn't know that by offering only a remanufactured inventory we were getting knocked out of contention for any of that business. We recognized that the profit margin is low on brand name items, but we could still use that profit for charitable works. By providing a full range of products, we could reach a much broader spectrum of potential customers.

By giving customers a choice—they could either realize the savings of the compatible products or stick with the brand name products—we significantly increased the size of our market. And we enhanced our own image. The addition of those products made us appear more legitimate to our target audience.

▦ Expanding Our Outreach

Sales growth from 2002 to 2003 was tremendous, increasing from $2,000 the first year to $180,000, all from in-house marketing. We had been handling all of the company's marketing ourselves, out of necessity, as well as the fact that one of our areas of expertise is marketing communications. We eventually realized that we were the best stewards of the company's brand anyway.

While we haven't outsourced our marketing, we have broadened the market we serve. As we've mentioned, Father Bernard's original focus was on helping nonprofits, churches, and schools primarily, because they, like the monastery, do important work with limited funds. His aim was to give them what they needed in the way of ink and toner at a lower cost. We agreed that these were important markets to serve, but we broadened our target audience to include the home and home-based business buyer, who are also cost conscious and likely to want to support our mission with their purchases. These segments have become the mainstay of our business. Although each sale is smaller than average, what it lacks in dollar amount per sale is made up in volume.

We also shifted our market position. Instead of portraying ourselves as the little guy competing with the major players—we as David, they as Goliath—we have tried to balance that little guy image with the sense that we're still in the same league as the national chains.

But back in 2003, we were still very focused on building our customer base. One major project that year was building a database of Catholic institutions within each major Diocese and Archdiocese in the country. Referencing a big Catholic registry, we entered each listing by hand, typing in the name of the institution, the appropriate contact person, address, phone number, and size. The work was arduous, but critical for our growth. We needed to be able to reach out to our core customer base quickly, easily, and regularly. This database would make that possible.

As we grew, we stopped typing in entries by hand and starting buying lists, but only after there was sufficient cash to support the list purchases. Never ones to rely on credit to buy needed products and services for the business, we routinely found ways to get what we needed with what we had. Sometimes that meant doing a task the hard way. We never shrugged our shoulders and moved on to a less onerous task, giving up on what we really needed. Rather, we found a way to get the information, or the support, or the vendor relationship we needed. We tried to make progress every day, but we sometimes lost sight of the great strides we'd already made, until someone pointed it out.

A close friend and contractor who visits the monastery frequently was doing some repair work on one of our offices a couple of years ago. He made a point to thank us for lifting the stress that he saw affecting his good friend, Father Bernard. Prior to our work with LaserMonks, the necessary balance of work and prayer was completely off-balance, with much of the stress landing square on the shoulders of Father Bernard, the Steward of Temporal Affairs for the abbey.

By the spring of 2004 the business was covering most of its expenses and those of the abbey and we saw the first glimmer of success. For us that meant ensuring that the monks had the food and shelter they needed, and that there was money available to donate in support of charities and individual good works worldwide. We were also able to see that because we were handling the business, the monks could continue their life of prayer without interruption, a gratifying feeling for all of monkhelpers.

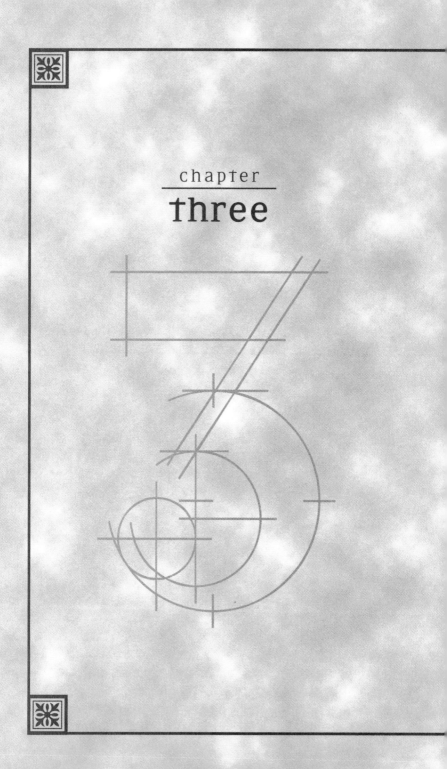

chapter
three

customer care and the rule of st. benedict

"**A**s the buyer of toner cartridges for my company, I get weekly calls from suppliers who want me to purchase their 'better than the other's' cartridges at their 'best price,'" says Dave Fleury of All Fasteners, Inc. in Franksville, Wisconsin. "They often want me to do a free trial or purchase more cartridges than I need. Often they are quite pushy."

"Well, I use LaserMonks as my way to prove that theirs isn't the best price. In almost every case I can pull up the LaserMonks Web site and tell them the price we get from you is cheaper. When I explain your charitable contributions as a result of our purchase and recycling, they don't pursue it any further," he says. "To put it another way, they don't have a prayer—and I mean that in several ways!"

We chuckled when we received this note from Dave and were heartened that he valued those very benefits LaserMonks tries to provide each customer every day. Our goal is to keep our product pricing low so that more individuals and companies save money—that's one part of our mission—but the other part is inviting others to participate in good works around the globe, something that is made possible through our customers' purchases. The way we involve our customers, and the way we treat everyone who comes in contact with LaserMonks is another way we try to distinguish the company.

The Cistercian monks follow The Rule of St. Benedict, which emphasizes the concept of hospitality; sharing everything they have, who they are, and what they value. Hundreds of years ago, the Cistercians and other orders of monks who followed The Rule, routinely invited guests to enjoy their hospitality. Back then, hospitality meant listening to the Word of God in community prayer, sharing their mealtime table, and experiencing monastic peace simply by being at the monastery.

Today, as laypeople running LaserMonks, we use The Rule as our guide to how we treat customers. We do our best to receive our customers with gracious respect and joyful service, whatever that might mean for each individual. And whether someone reaches out to us for the first time or is a longtime LaserMonks customer, we do our best to share our hospitality with them. In turn, they enrich our company and our community. They also help us discover and extend the boundaries of our love and concern, by making us aware of other people and organizations that can benefit both from our products and from our charitable giving.

Hospitality is a fluid term that is applied differently to each situation and each customer, sometimes surprising those who have not dealt with us before. Even customers who *have* dealt with us are sometimes shocked by the lengths to which we will go to serve them. It's all about hospitality.

▨ A 1,500-Year Tradition of Hospitality

A case-in-point is a customer who called us a few months ago complaining that one of our cartridges was stuck in her printer.

We looked up her order history and saw that she hadn't ordered from us in two years. It was unlikely she was still using those same cartridges she had purchased from LaserMonks. Consequently, it was equally unlikely that the cartridge stuck in her printer was ours.

But because LaserMonks is built on a foundation of care and hospitality, we listened while the woman described at length her call to the manufacturer of the printer. They told her that her five-year-old printer was no longer under warranty and that there was nothing they could do for her. She was livid.

So she called us to demand—not ask for, but demand—her money back for the cartridges. She was not interested in any of our suggestions for removing the cartridges to alleviate the problem, she just wanted her money back. She wanted satisfaction, and we realized that it was our job to turn an angry customer into a happy one. Which product or company was at fault was really irrelevant at this point for the customer. We had an opportunity.

"We're very sorry for the inconvenience this has caused you," we told her, "and we will replace the printer at no cost."

There was stunned silence on the other end of the line, followed by a much softer tone and attitude.

While she was still on the phone, we went to the printer manufacturer's Web site and found her printer, plus a newer version with more features, which we ordered for her. She was shocked, not only because we were willing to replace her printer, but also because we would go so far as to buy her an even better printer than the one she had been using.

By the end of the conversation, she was a Laser-Monks customer for life. "I am going to recommend LaserMonks to all of my friends and colleagues," she told us again and again.

What did it cost to earn the appreciation and loyalty of this new LaserMonks champion? A mere $125. Now, most business owners will undoubtedly ask why in the world would we buy a printer for someone when we weren't obligated to do so. And our response is, "How could we not?" She called us in need and we had the opportunity to help her.

That $125 investment will yield much more in sales from the referrals this customer will make, and for the word-of-mouth that will surely occur because of the hospitality she experienced.

This was an unusual situation. LaserMonks, like any business, does make mistakes from time-to-time. As an online merchant without a huge inventory at our location, we generally rely on drop-shippers to send out orders directly to our customers. Such relationships allow us to offer a much wider selection of products and to get purchases into customers' hands more quickly. But there have been times when the drop-ship companies make mistakes in packing and shipping the products. We have no control over it, but we are very aware that it reflects directly on LaserMonks.

With many online merchants, double shipments can occur, and LaserMonks is no different in that regard. Although there is an additional cost to us when this happens, our policy is to ask the customer to keep the extra shipment at no charge and with our blessing. Our goal is to turn a mistake into a positive experience for the customer, rather than causing them further inconvenience by asking them to box up the extra cartridges and ship them back to us. The damage to our relationship with the customer would never be worth it.

Although they don't always expect it, we always aim to satisfy any customer who reports a mistake or problem.

One small-business customer called a couple of weeks ago to place an order and then called back the following week asking to speak to a supervisor.

"I called last week to place an order and wanted you to know that you may want to consider moving the person who took my call to a job that would better suit her skill set," she told us, which was a nice way of saying she thought the worker shouldn't be in customer service.

"While she looked up the ink cartridge my printer needed she kept sighing and commenting how 'it had been a long day,' and made me feel I was inconveniencing her by asking her to help me. I thought you might want to know how your customers are being treated," she finished.

Of course, we did want to know how customers were being treated, but our first priority was helping the woman determine which supplies she needed so she could complete her order with us. After we did that, we talked with her about the qualities needed to succeed in a customer service role and how both our companies were founded on the principle of customer care.

We told her that her comments were much appreciated and that we took them very seriously. We said we would be taking action to improve our customer service process based on her input. She probably thought we were just trying to placate her, but we were serious.

The next day we contacted a company we had previously used for interpersonal training and arranged for a companywide workshop on connecting with customers by phone, and how to deal with challenging customers.

The workshop proved even more useful than we expected, mainly because we learned a number of things about the monkhelper who had had difficulty helping our customer. During the session, she talked about what affects the way she does her job and the way she approaches customers, admitting that during the past month she had been having a hard time at home. She was being challenged by family and health issues that were impacting her phone attitude and demeanor, and we hadn't known about it.

We realized she needed some special attention from us. In addition to giving her increased flexibility in her hours while she attended to the situation at home, we also saw a need to schedule frequent breaks for her during the day, so she could regroup and unwind between customer calls.

A week after the workshop, we called the customer again to let her know that we had all completed additional customer service training. Thanks to her observations and communication were able to identify a weakness in our system. She was sincerely shocked that we would take action based on her comments and that we would follow up with her about it.

"Good customer service isn't simply dealing well with customers, but also listening to customers when they encounter problems, and taking proactive steps to deal with situations needing attention," she told me. She was impressed that we did exactly that and she continues to buy from us today.

▓ Applying The Rule to Vendors

In studying The Rule of St. Benedict and working to apply it to LaserMonks, we realized that hospitality is about more than just how we treat our customers and our community. It also applies to how we deal with our vendors.

Working with vendors can be stressful. They are an integral part of our customer service process, yet in many ways we have little control over them. Accurate and speedy delivery is their main function and we spend time each and every day in phone and e-mail communication with our core vendors. To our customer, one mis-delivered product or incorrect shipment may taint their experience with LaserMonks, while to the vendor, one mistake out of hundreds of perfect orders is a record to be proud of. Our job is to balance our customers' needs with the respect we show our vendors who, by and large, do a superior job for us. However, mistakes do happen.

Among our list of vendors are other U.S. monasteries, which provide a number of items we use in our gift baskets, from bread to preserves to cakes to caramels and more. We learned long ago that monks run on a different clock than lay folks like us and we have definitely had to channel our inner St. Benedict when dealing with some of the monasteries.

Shortly after we introduced our gift baskets, right before the holiday season, we were deluged with orders. We had anticipated some of the increased demand and had ordered ahead in anticipation, but the number of orders were even greater than we had hoped and there seemed to be no end to the demand, so we ordered even more cases of products from the various monasteries in order to be able to put together and ship the baskets from the abbey in a timely fashion.

We received all the products we needed in plenty of time, except one. So we e-mailed the monastery to inquire about the shipment. No response. So we called and were promptly disconnected. When we called back, we were left on hold for a full 20 minutes.

We finally got an e-mail from a nun at the monastery apologizing for not having shipped the product, which we had already paid for, and eventually it was shipped. The reason she gave for the delay was that it was a training issue and the new person who was taking orders was not fully trained. Since the monastery had always had excellent customer service and never a shipping problem, we let it go without another thought. Surely this was an aberration.

Because of the huge influx of orders, soon after we needed to order more product from the same monastery. With two weeks until we had to ship the gift baskets from the abbey, we were confident this was plenty of time for them to send us our order. However, a few days before the gift baskets were due to be shipped, we realized that—again—we didn't have the order from the one monastery.

We called again and again got no response, and then e-mailed requesting a tracking number. Two more days passed before we heard from the nun, who apologized profusely. Another training issue had prevented our order from being processed and had interfered with anyone letting us know the order had not yet gone out. At this point, we were frustrated and angry and concerned that we wouldn't be able to ship all the gift baskets to our customers because this vendor hadn't paid attention.

A year earlier, we might have been less than gracious with the nun, but today, with an understanding and appreciation for The Rule of St. Benedict, we took a much more balanced approach. We suggested to the nun that perhaps people in training shouldn't be permitted to process orders until they are fully trained or, if they are permitted to process orders, they could have a more experienced person working with them.

Falling back on The Rule, we also tried to turn the situation around to help her feel less stressed. We let her know that this was a good problem to have—the higher than average orders—because it showed how much their product is loved by our customers, which is why we needed so much of it. After successfully resolving the issues on the phone and being assured by the nun that our order was being shipped immediately, we thanked the nun for personally taking care of this.

We also told her that we understood the challenge of monasteries running businesses—which is why laypeople run LaserMonks—and that if we could ever be of assistance, to please let us know.

Hospitality in our business is about more than how we treat our employees and customers, it's also about how we treat and care for all the people we come in contact with—the vendors that do our fulfillment, the UPS delivery driver, the company that supplies our phone system, and on and on.

▤ The Indirect Route to Customer Satisfaction

In Spring 2006 we had an interaction with another vendor that proved frustrating, and it also reminded us of the core principles of hospitality we strive to live by at LaserMonks. We had a customer in Alaska order a group of products that were to be shipped via second-day air. It wasn't a difficult request, but it was unusual enough that we thought we should call it in directly to the vendor rather than just sending it through our data interchange system.

When we called customer service we were told that the products were not available for shipping from the closest warehouse—Seattle—but had to be shipped from Albany, New York. This didn't sound like a problem until the customer service rep told us they could only ship to Alaska by barge from the Seattle warehouse. Now this sounded very odd to us, so we asked her to double-check with a supervisor about it. She came back a few minutes later and told us they simply couldn't fill our request.

We were perplexed. Of course UPS could air ship an order from any state in the United States to Alaska, but apparently some people at the vendor didn't understand this. Instead of arguing with the rep, which would have been our knee-jerk reaction since this was such a simple request, we thanked her for her help and hung up.

We then called another customer service rep at the same vendor whom we deal with routinely, but who we didn't think needed to be contacted for such an easy order. She took care of the order. It was shipped second-day air from Albany, New York, as we expected.

Now, whether St. Benedict would have approved of us going around one person to deal with someone else we can't be sure, but it saved the first customer service rep from grief and embarrassment and, more importantly, it solved our shipping problem for our customer.

▦ Incorporating The Rule into Modern Business

Fifteen centuries ago, a young monk named Benedict crafted a doctrine for balanced monastic living that formed the cornerstone of Western monasticism. It was written for monks—men who come together to live a life of contemplation and prayer in search of God—but its teachings can be applied much more broadly.

The Rule addresses the basic monastic virtues of humility, silence, and obedience and directs followers to set aside time daily for common prayer, meditative reading, and manual work. Its scope is both narrow and broad, that is, specific in its discussion of clothing, sleeping arrangements, food and drink, care of the sick, reception of guests, recruitment of new members, and journeys away from the monastery, but broad in its treatment of larger issues such as charity and Christian values.

During our early planning sessions regarding LaserMonks and its structure, we quickly realized that The Rule's tenets were appropriate for many organizations, not just monasteries. The Rule focuses on management—of individuals, lifestyle, and performance, for example—just as we, as leaders of Laser-Monks, were focused on managing its growth and success. The Rule deals with leadership of the Abbot and motivation and guidance of the monks within the community, giving us useful direction in how best to motivate and guide our helpers. We recognized that its teachings were an invaluable guide for LaserMonks and we have done our best to weave it throughout the business.

We also realized that The Rule has endured for centuries, having been interpreted by multiple monastic orders—Benedictines, Cistercians, Carthusians, Trappists, and others—and is clearly flexible enough to be applied to our organization. If each of the monastic orders could adopt The Rule and develop their own personalities and practices around it, so could we.

While we recognized that we lacked the background needed to teach The Rule to others, such as our helpers or our customers, we believed we could interpret the teachings and apply them to a modern business like LaserMonks.

In fact, with The Rule as our guide, developing our mission and vision statement was fairly simple; the guidelines and priorities were laid out so clearly for us 1,500 years ago.

▣ Working Together—A Literal Interpretation of The Rule

One of the key passages of *The Rule of St. Benedict* reads:

> *"Let all guests who arrive be received like Christ . . . Let the Abbot or the brethren meet him with all charitable service. And first of all let them pray together, and then exchange the kiss of peace . . . After the guests have been received . . . the greatest care and solicitude should be shown, because it is especially in them that Christ is received."*

We felt strongly from the beginning that this philosophy needed to be at the center of our customer-care approach, that everyone associated with Laser-Monks needed to understand how customers were to be treated. That meant finding a way to have our monk-helpers, subscribe to this philosophy. We started by developing our own interpretation of The Rule, based on our many conversations with the monks, as it relates to groups of people living and working closely together.

Our version of The Rule for LaserMonks was:

> *"To extend an awareness of how a community can live together on a daily basis in an organized manner, and with a balance, and provide for the various personality types and needs of the people in that community."*

Clearly, we left out some of the most significant tenets of The Rule, regarding the monks' common goal of searching for God, but we applied much of the dictates to the business' operations.

One of The Rule's strongest themes is working together as a community with a common goal, and having everyone understand that goal. We took this to heart and made sure from the outset that everyone contributing to LaserMonks' growth understood our common goal and mission.

We took St. Benedict's words about monastic living quite literally when dealing with the people who have helped build LaserMonks through the years. We refer to these people as our "community." As St. Benedict set forth, we work daily on the organization and management of the community, as a way of ensuring we are meeting the needs of that community.

We stress team-building, as we thought St. Benedict would in today's modern business world, and encourage everyone to feel that we are all part of the same family. We involve our monkhelpers in all aspects of the business; everything from writing training manuals, to developing customer service procedures, to charitable giving. We bring in motivational speakers to lead workshops for us all in team-building and community.

In addition to emphasizing the importance of working together as a team, or community, we also want them to feel connected to the monks' community and work. They need to recognize that the mission of LaserMonks is to support the monks' ministry and charitable giving. To build that relationship with the monks, we ask the monks to lead half-hour sessions for the helpers on many topics related to The Rule, the Cistercian tradition of charity, and their lifestyle. We also make sure that all our monkhelpers receive a tour of the abbey and have the opportunity to attend mass in the abbey chapel. And we make available a wide array of reading and listening materials on the Cistercians.

"Time, Talents, and Treasures"

One of the first lessons we ever learned at the abbey came through a conversation with Father Bernard regarding how the monastery applies The Rule of St. Benedict to the management of the monks.

He told us that, as God's creatures, we all have "time, talents, and treasures," and that one of the challenges for an Abbot or Prior of an abbey was to find that in each monk, and to help each monk develop those skills and special attributes.

We use that same approach with our monk-helpers—we try to learn what their individual talents are. For example, instead of coming up with lists of tasks and responsibilities to assign to each monkhelper, we first meet with them to find out what they feel their talents are and what type of role would make them most happy. Then we try to match their needs and skills to what LaserMonks needs in the way of support.

Just as The Rule addresses the concept of balance within the monks' community, we try to balance the needs and wants of our monkhelpers—what they envision as their perfect work day—and the needs of the business.

▦ A Holistic Approach to Our Community

We also work to provide balance for our helpers in their work and home life. This is our adaptation of *"ora et labora"*—work and prayer—a key component of The Rule. We make certain that schedules revolve around the needs of the individual families who work with us. It is a sort of extreme flextime program.

For example, if a mom who works with us needs to be home to supervise her children after school, but has a different schedule during school breaks and during the summer, we arrange her responsibilities around the family's needs. Or, if a helper is not a morning person by nature, we arrange for their work hours to be in the afternoon and early evening.

LaserMonks is located in a small, working class community, and many of our helpers are single mothers with several children to support. Years ago, when we began hearing that some of the monkhelpers didn't have enough food at home to feed their families, we began a weekly tradition we call "Raiding the Cabinets."

We weren't exactly sure how to offer food without having the helpers feel awkward about accepting charity, so we started by asking them to help us clear out the extra food we had on the shelves. This evolved into a weekly routine of clearing the cupboards of all canned and nonperishable food. We place the goods in bags and hand them out randomly to members of our community.

Around the holidays we always buy extra food—turkeys, hams, pie fixings, sacks of potatoes, anything else we can think of that people eat at the holidays—and we divide up the surplus and distribute it. We think St. Benedict would have approved.

🔲 Going Above and Beyond

While part of our mission has been to tend to the needs of our customers and our monkhelpers, we also recognize that caring for members of a community sometimes calls for more than simply providing food, clothing, and shelter, or a means to earn the money to pay for them. In addition to tending to the physical and emotional health of our community, we also try to listen between the lines to identify other unmet needs or wants we can help with.

Not only does it improve the worker's performance, more importantly, it validates their self-worth and boosts their self-esteem to know that someone is paying attention to what's important to them.

A few years ago we had a helper who was a huge country music fan. One day in conversation she mentioned that one of her dreams was to attend a country western concert. She had never been able to afford to take her children and herself—the tickets were just too expensive—but she hoped one day she might be able to. Little did she know that day was right around the corner.

The next week, much to her surprise, she received four tickets to a concert by a well-known country music star. But they weren't just any tickets, they were tickets for seats just feet from the stage. With tears in her eyes, her voice trembling, she told us those tickets were the nicest thing that anyone had ever done for her and her family.

Demonstrating that our monkhelpers are special and deserving is one way we work to build an organization that functions well. Going above and beyond providing payment for their time spent working is part of our culture. We're a community and community members all need to feel valued in order to perform at their best. We've proven through experience that workers will treat a customer the way they are treated at work, much the way a child will treat others the way they are treated at home.

The way we try to treat our helpers, with caring and respect, mirrors how the Cistercians deal with their own community members. Cistercians are compassionate and giving, always looking to spotlight the positive skills and attributes of fellow monks, instead of criticizing and pointing out weaknesses. We try to follow their lead in how they treat members of their community.

▦ How We Treat Workers Reflects Our Community's Values

Treating workers well reflects LaserMonks' values which, we hope, attracts like-minded customers. Our monkhelpers' enthusiasm for their work and their attitude about their workplace results in satisfied customers, which then benefits LaserMonks as an organization and brings The Rule full circle.

When a customer reaches out to a business by phone or e-mail, or steps into a retail storefront, the ensuing interaction speaks volumes about the workplace atmosphere. Our goal in emphasizing hospitality is for customers to share the balance and happiness of the monkhelpers and for the monkhelpers to share their positive experience at LaserMonks with customers.

By creating a warm, caring workplace where worker talents are as important as the tasks that need completing, and the identity of the worker is more than just a statistic, those same workers will increase the success of the business by creating customer care and hospitality that is memorable and quality-driven.

▦ Incorporating The Rule into Customer Care

Today, centuries after its creation, The Rule remains a charter by which monks worldwide continue to live. In addition, it provides guidelines for other organizations to follow as well. Though adapted for modern-day usage, the principles of The Rule remain a foundation of monasteries, universities, and a multitude of religious groups, not to mention LaserMonks.

Benedictine hospitality is marked by special attention being lavished on guests who spend time at the abbey. All visitors are met at the gates or door by the Abbot or his deputy, and are assigned a special monk caretaker who watches over their needs during their stay. This special care is fairly easy to visualize, but when you try to imagine what that level of attention would look like within a twenty-first-century business, the picture gets a bit fuzzy.

Our biggest challenge, as laypeople running a business owned by monks, was learning to incorporate these Benedictine principles into the company in a way that differentiated us.

So we made up a role-play exercise with our workers, which we called "The Twelfth Century Visitor." It was our way of trying to figure out how to apply St. Benedict's teachings to our modern-day venture. That is, taking contemporary customer service scenarios and applying twelfth-century hospitality based on The Rule.

The game is fairly simple, but encourages us all to consider how we would respond to various customer scenarios. We start by sitting in a circle, all of our monkhelpers and the two of us, and one person assumes the role of the visitor, another the Abbot of the abbey, and the rest play the other monks in the abbey.

We start with three sets of index cards, all pre-labeled. One set consists of the position of the various monks in the abbey, such as abbot, cellarer, deputy, etc. Another set consists of the types of visitors and their plight, such as a hungry visitor or a visitor in need of shelter for the night. And the third set consists of tasks that the monks are involved in at the time the visitor appears on their doorstep. For example, the monks might be in prayer, eating a meal, or sleeping in their cells.

The other side of each of the cards features the modern-day equivalent. For example, the hungry, complaining visitor from the twelfth century would be morphed into a twenty-first century irate customer who had received defective toner cartridges. The card featuring the monks in prayer, might, on the other side, have the entire LaserMonks team in a meeting when a customer called. And the twelfth-century monk who managed the abbey might be on the flip side of the card with the individual who manages the LaserMonks office.

By flipping over three of the cards, we are presented with a scenario we need to work through using role-play, guided by our roles on the cards. So, for example, one scenario might be a wandering nomad who hadn't eaten for days who happens upon the abbey. He simply needs a few good meals and shelter from the elements. We might add a twist and make the nomad deaf and very ornery. Then what would happen if the nomad arrived while the monks were in the middle of a meal or in prayer?

"How would St. Benedict want us to act?" is the main question posed by the game. What should the role of the abbot be? What can we do to make the visitor feel more welcome?

After role-playing the twelfth-century scenario, we then turn over the cards and replay the same situation as it relates to LaserMonks. Instead of a deaf, hungry nomad, we might be faced with an older, hard-of-hearing customer who is calling simply to ask if we carry a certain product.

And instead of being in the middle of prayer or a meal, how would we deal with the customer if he or she called right at the end of the day, eager to have a lengthy chat when we should be heading out the door?

We pose questions of the team to learn how each of us would handle the same situation, and if there is anything we as a company can do to improve the customer's experience. Would the customer's experience be any different if it were Cindy or Sarah versus the other monkhelpers? Would the helper be willing to stay past 5:00 p.m. to talk with the customer? Would the monkhelper be willing to stay past 5:15 p.m. that night? Later? What factors would make a difference?

What if the helper's child was home with a fever or the helper wasn't feeling well? Would the monkhelper be as willing to patiently chat with the customer?

The game helps us explore how we would handle various situations and brings up larger issues surrounding LaserMonks' reputation and how it is shaped by each customer's perception of our hospitality. We ask, "How does the treatment of one customer affect the company's image?" (If it's true that each of us knows 200 people, how would a positive experience potentially impact LaserMonks?)

Other questions that we tackle include:

- How can we recognize when a monkhelper isn't equipped to deal with certain customers?

- How can we face our shortcomings so that the customer does not suffer as a result?

- How can we understand the mindset of the customer?

• How can we make each person who reaches out to us feel special and welcome?

And, most important, how can we continue to develop our customer service and differentiate ourselves from other companies?

We've played this game many times through the years, spending countless hours learning about ourselves, The Rule and its application, and our customers. We've also made some discoveries along the way about how our different temperaments handle different customer personalities and situations, sometimes with comical results.

Although we frequently fall short of St. Benedict's model regarding customer care, we are comforted in the knowledge that as long as we always aspire to do better, we are certainly on the right track.

Can You Take Customer Care Too Far?

Just as the Cistercians adore Christ, we try to adore our customers, if not literally, then at least in spirit. And in that spirit of customer care, we have found that you can never give a customer too much service, too much care.

Our belief is that in every communication with a customer, whether via e-mail, snail mail, phone, or fax, we can never love or respect them too much. And we've learned through the numerous customer service training sessions we have been part of, few experts refute this position.

During one such customer service workshop, the presenter asked us all to describe the worst customer service experience we, as consumers, had ever endured. After we each told our frustrating, maddening, and disappointing tales, we all agreed that the common element in all the stories was the feeling that the customer service representative did not care about us at all. We were not at all important, was the sense we got. And yet, a little bit of listening and responding with kindness would have made all the difference to us. In every instance such a reaction would have turned the entire scenario around, all the workshop participants agreed.

Given that several of those "worst" experiences occurred long ago, it was very clear to us that a customer's contact with the customer service department is an opportunity to provide a memorable experience for them to tell their friends about. Conversely, if we did nothing and allowed poor customer service experiences to occur, the same situation would likely occur, only the customers' memory would be clouded by anger and the description of that interaction would be relayed to friends with a warning, not encouragement or delight. Either way, customers would tell others about their experience, so why not make it an extremely positive one.

We find that going overboard with customer service only results in an excellent experience for the customer. There is never a downside.

▨ Educate the Customer for an Improved Experience

Although we can tell customers that we are a different kind of company and that our mission is special, if we involve them in the process, they are much more likely to become advocates and champions than if we didn't. So part of our hospitality and customer care involves spending extra time on the phone with customers, discussing our featured charities of the month or discussing the good works that we are doing in our community or in the customer's community. We also ask them, our customers, what kind of good works they would like to see us add in the future, and we ask them about their benevolent experiences.

Our questions are a natural outgrowth of the conversation, which often include queries about the monks, or their history, or our life on the abbey property. And when we get any kind of media exposure, in the form of magazine or newspaper articles, or TV programs mentioning us, we often receive a large influx of calls. Many ask the same kinds of questions about the monks behind LaserMonks.

Through these experiences, we have learned that taking the time to answer questions from curious customers is even more important than noting what kind of ink cartridge they need to purchase. Their questioning us about the company is our opportunity to educate them about our mission, our work, and how they play a pivotal role in our ability to continue to do this important work.

However, we began to wonder whether indulging such curiosity was limiting LaserMonks' growth. We certainly want to treat each customer as St. Benedict would have, and to be knowledgeable about our products in order to help them, but from time-to-time, we receive phone calls from customers who seem to be more interested in the monks themselves than in making a purchase. Should we cut short such phone calls when it is obvious the person on the other end is not a serious customer?

We asked ourselves, "How do we handle curious customers who want to talk for long periods of time?" Which was more important, making the sale or assuaging the curiosity of consumers who wanted all sorts of information about our operations and our home? And "How do we handle customers who call in claiming to be God?" Believe it or not, it has happened.

Late one afternoon, soon after we started answering phones for LaserMonks, we picked up an interesting call. We asked all the typical questions we ask of a new customer, finding out what sort of printer he or she needed replacement cartridges for and adding those things to the shopping cart. Things were going as usual. When the time came to set up a customer account, the customer stated his name was "God." First and last: "God God." It might have been our inclination to laugh, or to question him, but professionalism is really first and foremost in our minds.

When the account was set up we fully expected when the time came to enter a credit card, that a different name would be used. Not true. The order went through without a hitch, and was shipped off to God.

From time to time since then we have donated various cartridges to God.

We are not sure if when the monks started this business that it was part of their business plan to sell to God, but at times we laugh to each other about it and say, "Look how far we have come!"

Ultimately we decided that part of LaserMonks' appeal is its unique business model and its unique connection to monks, who are a curiosity to most people because of their lifestyle. People are simply curious about monks and about us and about how we run the business. And, believe it or not, it has been beneficial at times to let the second phone line ring a time or two more in order to continue a conversation with a customer whose brother is a priest, or who is intrigued by the monks and their lives.

Balancing the need for sales to sustain the business with the principles of hospitality and The Rule can be challenging at times, but we simply remind ourselves that LaserMonks' mission is different, as are its priorities. Although a typical for-profit company might not spend as much time on the phone with its customers, caring for callers and letting them know that we value them is critical to the way LaserMonks operates.

Train Customers to Expect Superior Customer Care

Just as we try to teach our customers about the benefits of doing business with LaserMonks, we have also worked hard to teach them what to expect from us. That means providing some sense of what The Rule is all about; providing a level of customer care that St. Benedict would have been proud of.

Of course, setting and maintaining such high expectations of ourselves and our team isn't easy. In fact, we constantly look for ways to improve our customer care department and the level of service customers should expect.

One way that we evaluate how well we're doing toward achieving 100 percent customer delight is by asking. We love asking our customers about their experiences with LaserMonks. We hear back from them in e-mails, phone surveys, and in normal conversation.

But we also have more formal processes for assessing our performance, such as the phone survey of 250 randomly selected customers we did a few years ago. Through the survey we heard that 98 percent of our customers rated our customer care as excellent and, in general, were very happy with our products and services. But what did that tell us? What could we learn from this information? Not much.

We realized that rather than pat ourselves on the back for satisfying 98 percent of our customers, we needed to dig deeper into the two percent who had a less-than-stellar experience. So we contacted those customers (that we knew about) who had encountered problems in their dealings with us. They may have had defective products delivered, or received their delivery later than promised, or had some other disappointment with our products or services. This survey told us what we needed to focus on to continuously improve our customer service.

Now we conduct a quarterly survey of all our customers who may have been less-than-pleased with their LaserMonks experience. Sometimes it is painful to hear the comments, but it certainly drives home the need to overshoot the mark in terms of customer care.

Following the example of St. Benedict, customers enrich our company and our community, which helps us extend the boundaries of the care we provide others. It's an unending circle. The more we do to care for customers, the more they care for LaserMonks, which enables us to do more for the community at large.

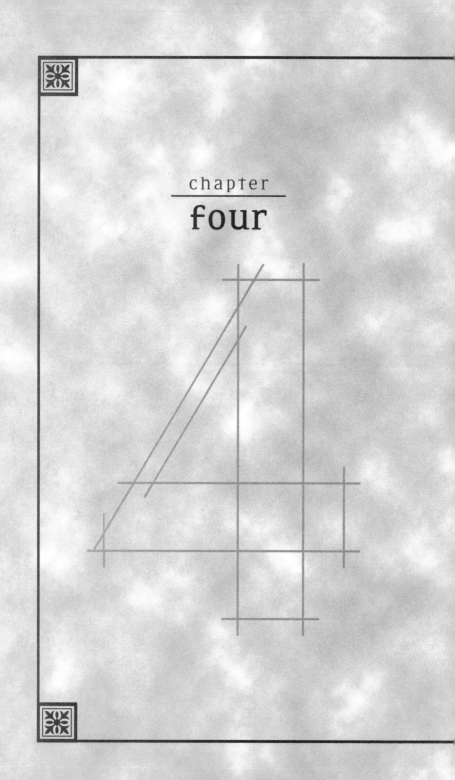

chapter
four

giving is good business

ONE OF THE BRIGHT SPOTS OF THE SUMMER
OF 2005 FOR THE CHILDREN OF A POOR NEIGH-
BORHOOD IN ST. PAUL, MINNESOTA, WAS THE
WEEKEND BETHLEHEM LUTHERAN CHURCH HELD
ITS HAMLINE MIDWAY GIVEAWAY AND STREET
FEST. ONE FAMILY IN PARTICULAR WAS ESPECIALLY
TOUCHED, AND THEIR MOTHER, A SINGLE MOM
LIVING WITH HER CHILDREN IN A LOW-INCOME
APARTMENT WITH SPORADIC HEAT AND WATER,
HAS A VIVID MEMORY OF THE STREET FEST.

It was there that her children were given backpacks filled with school supplies—supplies that they would have gone without had the church not started its outreach program, and had LaserMonks not supported it.

In addition to the much-needed backpacks, we also provided the church with funds for hot dogs and hamburgers, chips, and soda for residents to enjoy for lunch. For many it was the only meal they had that day.

When we became involved in running Laser-Monks, supporting charitable efforts like Street Fest was not optional, it was a business imperative. Having funds to invest in community good works was more important than marketing and advertising. We opted not to spend in those areas, which we deemed non-essential, in order to have more money to improve people's lives, which we deemed *was* essential.

That decision shaped how the business is run and how it has grown.

▣ Helping Others Help Others

In its second year in business, after redefining the company as a socially conscious enterprise, Laser-Monks "reinvested" 100 percent of its profits in good works. We didn't distribute them to management or reward employees with huge bonuses, as most for-profit ventures do. Instead, we gave all the money left over after expenses to individuals, families, and organizations in need.

Those organizations included formal charities like Faith in Action, as well as not-so-formal efforts, like sending a nurse from Wisconsin to Louisiana to treat victims of Hurricane Katrina, and schools and churches in Wisconsin, and beyond. LaserMonks has also served the needy in Vietnam and Croatia, thousands of miles away from the monastery. Their location really isn't important. What is important is that they needed help.

So why would a business—a for-profit enterprise—give away all the money it worked so hard to earn? We do it because philanthropy reflects our goals for the business and our core mission—"to help others help others." The more money we make, the more we can benefit people in need. And the truth is that the more money we've given away, the more customers we've attracted.

Our experience supports recent research. According to a 2002 Cone Corporate Citizenship Study, today's consumers want to make a difference with their purchases. Whether they're buying ink and toner cartridges or other products, if given a choice, consumers would rather support a socially conscious company. Price and quality being equal, 84 percent of Americans would be likely to switch brands to support good works. Eighty-four percent!

More recently, a 2006 online survey conducted by Cone, Inc. and AMP Insights, reported that 61 percent of thirteen to twenty-five-year-olds "feel personally responsible for making a difference in the world." Of those, 81 percent have volunteered in the last twelve months, 69 percent consider a company's social environmental commitment when deciding whom to buy from, and 83 percent will trust a company more if it is socially responsible.[1]

We think we're onto something big. But in the beginning, all we had was a vision, and not much else.

We did, however, have the guidance of the monks, and the teachings of the Bible. Although we live in the secular world and the monks live primarily in the sacred, we have tried to follow their teachings and tenets as best we can in managing LaserMonks. While we don't have ongoing, regular contact with the monks, when we do meet with them, we find their insights to be life-altering.

One such meeting occurred early in the history of LaserMonks, as we spoke with Brother Matthew, a monk who straddles both the secular and sacred worlds. A former Chicago cop who is married with a family, Brother Matthew was the oblate at the monastery until recently becoming a Deacon in the Diocese of La Crosse. An oblate can best be described as a person offered to the service of, and/or living in a monastery, but not under monastic vows or full monastic rule. An oblate can be a lay member of any of the various Roman Catholic societies devoted to religious work.

We were trying to figure out how to explain to our customers the rationale behind LaserMonks' work, the fact that we give away our proceeds to help

---

[1] http://www.usatoday.com/news/nation/2006-10-23-gen-next-cover_x.htm

others. And during one of our talks, Sarah told Brother Matthew about a saying her father always had: "If I had $10 in my pocket, I would first take care of my family, buying the food, shelter, clothing, and other necessities, and then I would give the remainder to my neighbors, our community, and the rest of the world, in that order." Brother Matthew observed that the Bible passage about Christian charity mirrors that approach: first take care of your family, then your neighbors—those close to you, your local community—and then the rest of the world.

He said, "A basic interpretation is that the person must care for his or her spouse, children, and close family first, and then these actions trickle down to the larger community. It would be a denial of one's moral obligation if their kids were hungry at home and the parent went off to volunteer at the soup kitchen," he explained.

Charity typically refers to "acts of benevolence and mercy for the poor and suffering," according to *The World Book Encyclopedia*. *World Book* adds, "In a larger sense, it is a feeling of goodwill for all mankind."

At its core, Judeo-Christian charity—which LaserMonks aims to follow—is about giving to others, about sharing the bounty with those who have less. That's exactly what we have done from day one; share everything the business has, even when it wasn't much, to benefit our families, our neighbors, our community, and the less fortunate in other parts of the world.

▓ Visualization Shapes the Business

Imagine the perfect tennis game. Visualize where the tennis ball should land. Imagine your legs bent correctly, your arms and body positioned at a precise angle, and your arms moving in a firm, even stroke. Your racquet, simply an extension of your arm, connects with the ball, sending it across the net.

Before you master "the perfect shot," you picture in your mind what it would look like, what it would feel like. Visualize hitting the ball perfectly every time. With practice, and over time, you will figure out how to work back from that visualization to find the areas of your game that bear improvement or alteration. We use this visualization when we play tennis, and we use this same technique in developing LaserMonks' charitable focus. We determine our ultimate goal and from there create the methods and means to arrive at that goal.

When Father Bernard first conceived of a company that distributed its profits to the needy, we didn't know there was a formal name for such an organization. We also weren't exactly sure how it would work. What we did know—what we could picture— was what the operation would look like. We effectively visualized our new business model; the socially conscious enterprise. Then we worked back from that picture to design it.

One tool we developed early on was the basic tenets of our "giving is good business" model. We still have our first draft hanging in our office. It reads:

- Do not look at charity as something inconvenient in the business—charity needs to be the "necessity."

- No dollar figure for good works—start with what we can afford to do daily and as the business grows, good works grow.

- Creativity is the key to giving.

- Get everyone involved.

- "Help others, help others."

- Make purchasing a "feel good" experience for customers.

- Success is measured by how much we can help our communities.

- Keep expenses low, charitable works high.

- Benevolence begins with one person.

- Those who can give are blessed.

- Lead by example: Teach other businesses to be socially conscious.

Although the amount we are now able to donate is much larger than what we had starting out, the basic operational process is the same.

⌧ Embedding Charitable Works into Daily Operations

Back when LaserMonks was processing just a few orders a day, with very little leftover to put food on the table at the abbey, much less to fund good works, we agreed that it was important to do whatever donating we could. We established giving as a priority, not the amount given. We decided that what we had, even if it was $10, was enough to do some good somewhere.

That's how it all started.

Sometimes we gave canned goods to a local shelter, other times we gave cash to a needy person on the street or to a monastery somewhere else that was experiencing hard times. The point was to give as much as we possibly could, even if the dollar value of our giving seemed trivial, to get into the habit of looking for opportunities to make a difference, no matter how small.

Starting small was critical, we felt, because we knew if we started practicing social consciousness, supporting charitable works, when we had so little to give, then it would be so much easier to continue on that path if and when LaserMonks became as successful as we hoped it would.

Since the opportunities to help seem unending, we put a priority on projects that would support people doing charitable works to benefit others. Sort of the "pay it forward" model. But we also like helping people help themselves, too.

Back in 2004, Father Bernard was visiting Los Angeles and made a side visit to minister to an extremely poor area of Mexico. While he was there he met a remarkable man who was paralyzed from the waist down. Despite being so clearly disadvantaged, handicapped, and living in this remote and impoverished community, the gentleman was determined to find a way to support his family—his mother, two siblings, and himself.

What he really wanted to do was to start a key-making business, cutting house keys, office keys, car keys—you name it—but he didn't have the means to get started. The family had survived on the charity of others and his mother's frugality, but having a marketable trade would help tremendously.

Father Bernard immediately saw the potential to change not only this man's life, but his family's, too. So he headed online to eBay and bought a key-making machine and plenty of key blanks and delivered them to the speechless recipient.

By providing the tools for this man to support himself, we were able to impact the lives of at least five people. Due to the remoteness of their location, they were unlikely to have gotten that sort of help from outsiders. The hope and autonomy the gift offered the family was as important as any future monetary gain they may see. It was a perfect example of helping others help themselves.

Our stated mission is "helping others help others." That was clearly the case in 2005 following Hurricane Katrina. LaserMonks sent thousands of dollars worth of products to help the hurricane victims, but that was just the beginning.

As part of our research into which organizations and people to support in the hurricane's wake, we discovered a church in Texas that was sheltering victims and assisting those on the Texas-Louisiana border. We planned to send a package to support the church's work, and we asked a local elementary school to have students write letters of hope to accompany the shipment.

Despite the fact that our town has only 8,500 residents and this particular school serves low-income families, we received dozens and dozens of letters of support from the kids. We were so touched that this Midwestern community, with very limited financial resources, would invest so much time and effort into letting the children of Katrina know that they cared. They were sincerely concerned about the welfare of the children a thousand miles away.

Here are a couple of the letters, exactly as they were written:

Dear Children,

We are sorry that your houses got broken and your trees blew away. We are sorry Hurricane Katrina hurt you. Have fun going to school in Texas and remember to be safe.

—Lawrence Lawson Elementary
and Mrs. P's Kindergarten class

Dear Friend,

My name is Cheyenne. I am a third grader. I live in Sparta, WI. I am sorry you had to move to a different state. I hope you feel better and feel safe in your new home. I hope that you meet some new friends. I hope you get the things that you need. Maybe someday you and your family will be able to move back. I am sorry that the hurricane did so much damage to your houses. I hope you are o.k.

Sincerely,

Cheyenne

Cheyenne's card had the words "Have Faith" on the outside, accompanied by a drawing of a pretty house and a rainbow. She clearly wanted to send a message of hope and she took a considerable amount of time preparing it.

Even more surprising was the $1,000 that the students and their families donated to support the Red Cross's efforts. They had so little, yet they gave generously.

▦ Involving Others

In addition to funding programs that allow people to help the less fortunate, we have also introduced a number of operational policies and procedures to make us more aware of the many opportunities to help others.

We try to follow the monks' lead by thinking about three human areas of need: the mind, body, and spirit. We use that triad as a guideline in our giving. We also look for ways to benefit multiple people or organizations in need through one donation.

For example, we support other monasteries by purchasing their products. We then feature these items on LaserMonks.com, where our customers can purchase them. The profits from sales of these monastery goods are donated to charities in need. In this way we not only support the various monasteries and religious organizations by purchasing their goods, but we support other charitable causes with the profits from resale.

We also encourage customers to recycle with us. When they do, we give 100 percent of the proceeds of our recycling efforts to charity. So, in addition to helping reduce landfill waste, customers are also supporting charitable works.

Every month we choose a Charity of the Month. We announce it on the LaserMonks Web site, and the charity receives all the proceeds from a particular initiative, such as recycling. During the holidays we choose several, and they are all featured prominently at the site and referenced in any publicity. Visitors to the site are reminded frequently which organizations are that month's focus.

We created a program called Random Acts of Kindness, in which customers get discounts for sending in stories of acts of kindness. We also practice random acts of kindness ourselves, giving customers the chance to choose which charity we donate to next. The customer could be calling in for any reason— placing an order, returning an item, or just inquiring about a product. At the end of the call, we let the customer know that we are donating a sum of money to one of several charities and we ask them to select one. Most customers are pleasantly surprised by this, though we have had some folks who were quite leery, wondering what the catch was—were we overcharging them, tacking on a charitable fee, or was there some fine print they had missed that forced them to donate money. There is no catch, we reassure them, but it's not every day that a corporation tells its customers that it is giving away money on behalf of the customer.

Closer to home, we have given money to some of our workers who were interested in starting their own businesses, and we've funded ideas that they have had for assisting local charities.

To ensure that we are constantly expanding our program of giving, we set aside fifteen minutes a day to brainstorm new ideas and approaches. During these fifteen minutes, we let voicemail answer the phone, and we focus solely on new ways to do good works. It's one of the only times when customers will have to wait a minute for a return call—it's that important to us and to the business.

Getting Employees Involved

One of our philosophies is involving our helpers and business partners in the good works decisions that are at LaserMonks' core. Of course, as a small business this is easier than within a major corporation, but it can certainly be done no matter how many employees you may have.

In addition to helping them see firsthand the result of their hard work, involving everyone in the giving process also instills team building and enables them to speak with conviction about the good works LaserMonks does every day—they've seen it, and they've done it.

Last year a local family's house burned practically to the ground, including just about everything they owned. Fortunately, none of the family members—including six children ranging in age from infancy to fourteen—was hurt, but they were left with nothing.

After reading in the newspaper about the family's plight, we put two LaserMonks helpers in charge of getting them what they needed. Working together, the helpers contacted the reporter who had written the newspaper article to find out what the family needed most. We gave the helpers a lump sum to buy whatever they decided made the most sense. They bought the family many things, from canned goods to toys and books, and then dropped the package off at a non-profit group that passed everything along to them.

Getting your employees involved teaches them about benevolence and helps them understand the tenets of a socially-conscious business. One of our helpers said that it really taught her kids to be aware of the needs of others in our community.

In addition to putting helpers in charge of serving those who are less fortunate, we also decided that we wanted to develop mini-LaserMonks models, that is, helping others to start companies with a similar social mission.

We felt the best way to do this was to start with the people who currently help us, to see if they had entrepreneurial aspirations. Our first investment was in a small business idea one of our helpers and her children developed.

They researched groups they might want to donate to and then came up with a business plan for their venture. We advised them to "Start with some-thing you know," which is what they did. They decided to design and make Advent calendars, with candy taped on each day, which they had been doing for years during the holidays. Only this year, instead of giving a few calendars away to friends and relatives, as they had in the past, they made many extras and sold them, donating the profits to a local organization that helps families in need.

A year later, they still talk about that experience and how good they felt after helping others by using their talents.

▨ The Charitable Marketing Plan

What made all the donations possible was customers; customers who were eager to buy from us once they understood their payment helped to support good works worldwide. The key there was simply telling our customers—putting it right in front of their faces. That was our marketing strategy.

We did this by explaining our model of giving the business's profits away to the needy. We put the message front-and-center on our Web site, we mention it in e-mails, and we talk about it when people call LaserMonks. We make sure prospects and customers understand where their money is going, and how their purchase will make a difference beyond refueling their laser printer with toner.

Our marketing message emphasizes the high quality of our product; our customer hospitality, based on a 1,500-year tradition; our low cost; *and* the fact that the customer's money goes to help others.

It's a very basic idea at the heart of our marketing plan. "Social entrepreneurism" and "civic responsibility" are not new terms, but rarely do you hear them associated with a for-profit venture.

▨ The Triple Bottom Line

Businesses that are struggling for survival may have a hard time imagining donating to charity. Without a steady stream of revenue to cover the rent, employee salaries, utility costs, taxes, and so on, how can a company set aside funds for charitable works?

LaserMonks did it by turning the equation around. Instead of seeing what was left over for good works, we defined "charitable works" as a main expense after sustenance of the abbey. Once the abbey covers its operating expenses, the money left over is used to support good works.

During our leaner times, we decided that first we would cut out all expenses unrelated to keeping the abbey and the business running. That meant no advertising dollars, or marketing, for that matter. No employee bonuses, corporate jets, or slush funds. No fluff. If we had a dollar to give, we gave it, and we let customers know that their purchases helped us give that dollar away to someone in need.

Of course, this model frequently raises eyebrows. During our early growth period, we had people from many different companies and industries offering us advice. One discussion was particularly memorable and underscored how we were different from most businesses.

We were on a conference call with a prestigious consultant who catered to the corporate upper echelons, as well as his analyst and business manager. The trio had offered to give us advice on how we should be growing LaserMonks.

During the call we talked about everything—profits, growth, expansion, marketing methods, and pursuing corporate clients. Most of the talk centered on the bottom line and profit margins—the typical focal point of most for-profit businesses.

We listened politely to these esteemed consultants, not wanting to appear ungrateful or impolite, but finally we had to speak up.

"We're actually taking a different approach," we explained. "We're reversing the typical business model, using good works as our bottom line rather than profits."

There was stunned silence on the other end of the line.

"But you have to have a profit margin bottom line," the analyst protested. "You simply can't give money to good works before other necessary expenses like advertising or travel and entertainment," added the business manager. "Instead of giving money to needy organizations, you should be spending it on hiring business consultants and putting money toward trying to procure corporate contracts or hiring an outside sales force," the consultant explained.

Clearly they didn't comprehend *our* model. In our model, benevolence is the marketing fuel that makes

LaserMonks more successful. We don't need to set aside money for marketing, or budget for it, because the money allocated for good works is our marketing. It certainly costs us money to donate school supplies to a needy family or to a parish school in need, but this cost is offset by the new business it generates when the recipients relate their good experience with Laser-Monks. The call from a new business owner who asks us about our prices and finds out we are willing to donate their first ink order to them as they get their business up-and-running will also generate revenue in the long run. This philosophy brings us far more business than the cost of the products we give away. The groups we give to become our marketing partners, in effect, helping to publicize the company for us.

According to master salesman Joe Girard, who created the Sales Law of 250, each of us know approximately 250 people. We believe this figure is important and this belief is at the core of our growth pattern. Each time we interact with someone—a prospect, a customer, a charity, a parish, a person in need—we are tapping into their network of 250. Each time we help a worthy cause we are also increasing our business.

⁕ The More You Buy, The More We Give

It took us a while to quantify the LaserMonks growth equation, but here it is at its most basic level:

1. When an individual or group purchases from LaserMonks, proceeds go to initiate and support good works.

2. Therefore, it follows that the more customers buy, the more they are helping others.

3. The more customers buy, the more successful our business becomes, and the stronger our negotiating position in asking for better pricing from our vendors, which then yields more money to give to good works.

4. And the more money we save nonprofit organizations, churches, schools, and other charitable groups, the better stewards they are of their funds and the more money they have available to help others.

It's such a simple model, but it works. It works well.

▓ A Small Budget Can Still Yield a Big Impact

Any business can follow this business model by starting small, as we did. Instead of throwing the lavish annual Christmas party, for example, complete with catered dishes and flowing liquor, take that money and fund a project that gets your employees involved in a local charity. Or instead of an employee golf outing, take the budgeted money and direct it toward a local organization in need, with employees spending a day volunteering at the charity instead.

You can also spend less on traditional marketing methods and set aside some of that money to donate to charity. Then let your customers know their hard-earned money is going to do good work.

Challenging your employees to think of creative ways for your organization to give can generate a much broader list of opportunities to consider. Not to mention teaching everyone about benevolence. You'll also learn so much more about your workers; their pet projects, personal interests, and charitable organizations they already support outside of work. And by choosing to direct funds to agencies and charities your employees support, you'll reinforce your business's ties to its workers—an inexpensive way to increase employee retention.

Or, surprise an employee with a lump sum of money and ask them to use that money to fund a project where the proceeds go to charity. We did that, giving $1,000 to an area school and challenging them to come up with a charitable program. We were surprised by how much time and energy the kids invested in coming up with possible ideas, evaluating their options, and then developing a full-blown business plan, which they presented to Father Bernard.

They ultimately decided to participate in a walk for the Celiac Association, using the $1,000 to promote it in the hopes of raising far more than $1,000 to donate to the charity.

Customers can even be encouraged to become part of the process. Motivate them to tell you about their experiences with benevolence, and reward them for telling you. Not only will you strengthen your connection to the customer, but you'll encourage them to continue doing good works. Another win-win.

When customers support a business, as they do LaserMonks, with their continued purchases and referrals, the organization grows and succeeds. What you do with the additional cash flowing in is up to you. Led by the monks of Our Lady of Spring Bank, we have found the opportunity to share our success beneficial in so many ways.

Choose Your Good Works Carefully

The first step in becoming a socially conscious business is to state that as your goal and to make the commitment in your mind and in your business plan. Once you've clarified your mission and vision to be a socially conscious enterprise, you need to decide what kinds of people and organizations you want to help. There are so many groups out there in need, and many will ask for your help. Before deciding, think through what kinds of organizations speak to you. If you try to help all of them, you can quickly run through all of your available funds. That may be okay with you, but until you develop your criteria and plan for giving, you may feel overwhelmed by the opportunities before you.

Here are some tips for sorting through the many organizations and ways to support them:

- Decide whether you want to donate products/services or cash.

- Look for organizations that match the personality of your business, perhaps based on the products/services you specialize in, or on your target market.

- Think through whether you'd like to support many organizations with a small amount, or whether you'd rather have ongoing relationships with a few groups.

- Prepare a statement outlining the types of organizations you will and won't support (if any).

- Develop an application or form organizations need to complete in order to receive donations.

- Before handing over a check, do a little research on each applying organization to see what percent of each donation goes to covering overhead expenses and what percent actually goes to helping those in need.

- In return, ask for anecdotes or stories about how your money has helped that organization.

▨ Separating Wheat from Chaff

Establishing clear guidelines and expectations up front helped us deal with the onslaught of requests we began receiving. We were novices at social entrepreneurship and at first it was challenging to weed through all the statements of need, to determine which groups were in greatest need at any particular time.

We discovered that organizations needed assistance in all forms, from monastery help to ink and toner for their printers to basic necessities like food and clothing.

We also had people ask us for personal donations, everything from help getting utilities turned back on to buying someone a car to assisting with medical bills.

Setting up clear guidelines for donations and making them readily available to everyone asking for help finally cut down significantly on the random requests we received. First and foremost, we explained, we only donate to registered 501(c)3 nonprofits. Anyone asking for money directly from us was then encouraged to approach their local church or other nonprofit, who could in turn, make a formal request.

Of course, there are exceptions. We make sure we help our local community, and often that means giving private donations to families in need. When requests come in from schools asking us to help indigent families with school supplies, we never refuse them. Those are the types of good works that are important to us and to the business.

With Cistercian tradition as our guide, we divide LaserMonks' good works into three main areas: mind, body, and spirit. Limiting our focus to those three areas has also made it easier to sift through donation requests that have to do on some level with education, health, and spirituality.

Once your business has determined its charitable focus, whether it's mind, body, spirit, or supporting a particular type of nonprofit, such as Juvenile Diabetes or the United Negro College Fund, consider beginning your work locally.

▓ Balancing Business and the Desire to Do Good Works

It's easy to get caught up imagining the many ways you can have a positive impact on your community, because there are a million ways to do good works. But we caution business owners to take it step-by-step, rather than trying to achieve too much too soon.

This is exactly what we told a business owner who contacted us to help him with his new business. He wanted to model his business after LaserMonks, on a smaller scale initially, where he donated a portion of his profits to charity. And he started by asking a very good question about drop shipping. He wanted to use our drop ship model and, simultaneously, benefit a local shelter that was willing to take care of order fulfillment for his company.

Since his goal was to help as many in the community as he could, this scenario potentially offered the opportunity to do just that—provide income for the shelter while growing his business. But he asked us whether using the shelter for drop shipping was a smart decision.

As we tried to help him find an answer, we asked him many questions.

- Did the shelter have a track record of drop shipping? Had they done this before?

- If so, can they provide references?

- Was there another way that you could assist the shelter besides handing over customer shipments (such as donating a percentage of your profits or assisting with food or clothing)?

- How important was it to the business to have his customers be very satisfied with the accuracy of shipping and delivery?

As we went through the questions and answers, he came to the conclusion that as important as it was to assist those in need in his community, it was equally important to provide his customers the best and most accurate products and delivery. Using the shelter for order fulfillment would only add further complications to his business processes when there were many other creative ways he could help the shelter. So he opted to use a different drop shipping vendor.

LaserMonks runs into similar situations all the time.

Over the years, we have been approached by several charitable groups asking to be our distribution source. While we support and assist many of these groups in various ways, we have come to realize that using a national distribution channel is the best way to transact business and thus be able to put more money back into the charities.

That does not mean that in the future we may not incorporate such an organization into our daily operations. Just as the monks face challenges of balancing abbey sustenance with prayer for the world, LaserMonks is challenged with keeping the business strong and serving those in need.

What we have learned from running LaserMonks is that there is a balance between the business decisions we have to make and the people and organization we wish to help. Sometimes it's a difficult balance to strike.

▦ Good Works Begin Locally

When we started our good works program, we learned to take small steps, just as we had in building the business. Why not start by helping those in need in your community, and then fan outward to other communities later, like the branch of a growing tree. Starting locally will enable you to witness the result of your donations and help you hone your company's mission and scope before expanding it nationally and even internationally.

But don't just wait for organizations to contact you with their requests. Take a proactive approach and call on local nonprofit groups, clubs, schools, churches, and social service agencies and find out what they need most. Identify organizations that can benefit most from your help and consider establishing an ongoing relationship with some. We have several that receive regular support from us.

LaserMonks is located in a small town in Wisconsin, where many of the residents are families—many single moms with young children—who are close to the poverty level. We see the positive impact our good works have on the community first-hand.

We support many projects that help the local community, by donating several times a year to the local Boys and Girls Clubs, and working closely with shelters for the abused. In 2006 we sponsored a day to benefit the shelter—we set up cash boxes on retailer counters and alerted the community that all the money would go to support the shelter. We also sponsored the purchase of silicone bracelets that were sold in local stores, with all the proceeds going to the shelter and the families staying there.

Scholarships for local students are another great way to make an important contribution. And once you demonstrate your social consciousness, you may be surprised by how much your standing increases. Your community will embrace you. As a role model, you will encourage and inspire other local businesses to follow in your footsteps, too. The amount you set aside for these good works is much less important than your taking the first step and stating your commitment to support your community.

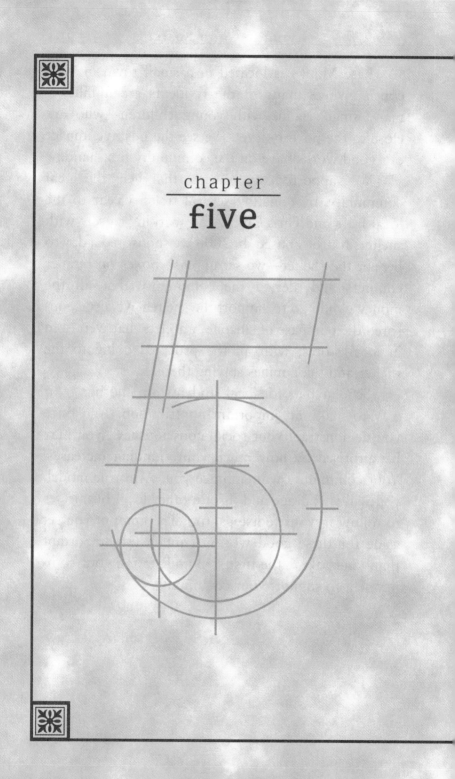

chapter
five

social
entrepreneurship
as a
marketing tool

"I HEARD ABOUT YOUR COMPANY FROM A FRIEND HERE IN THE MIDWEST AND I'D LIKE TO ORDER SOME INKJETS FOR MY PRINTER," THE MAN ON THE PHONE TOLD CINDY ONE MORNING NOT TOO LONG AGO. HE ASKED ABOUT THE VARIOUS CHARITIES WE SUPPORT AND THE OTHER GOOD WORKS WE DO. SINCE HE SEEMED SINCERE AND WOULD LIKELY BE HONEST WITH HER, SHE DECIDED TO ASK HIM A QUESTION.

"If you had a choice of purchasing your ink down the street at a national chain's store or through the mail from LaserMonks, who would you rather purchase from and why?" she queried.

"There is no question, I would buy from Laser-Monks," he responded immediately. "Even if the Laser-Monks' product was more expensive, I would much rather give my money to an organization that supports helping people," he explained.

He then went on to encourage us to increase our prices, as he believed most people would pay higher prices because of what LaserMonks is and does. He also validated what LaserMonks' message has been—that it is good business to give to others. Not only will this new customer continue to buy from us, but he will continue to spread word of our company just as his friend had done.

▨ You Can't Afford *Not* to Be Socially Conscious

We are all part of "the global village" now, whether we like it or not. Not only are we more aware of challenges people in other countries face, but we are also more closely connected to them. They are not faceless people in distant lands but people who we may be able to see, and whose story we may come to know. Thanks to the Internet and all the details it conveys, we see the world a bit differently than before the dawn of the Information Age.

In the past few years, consumers have become more aware of the availability and importance of supporting causes that benefit others. For some, that has meant a raised consciousness about environmental issues. For others, that has meant a raised awareness about food shortages in other parts of the world, or apartheid, slave labor, and blood diamonds.

Companies that offer a way to support efforts to right wrongs, or channel resources to the needy, are rapidly gaining ground. Just look at businesses that have designed and produced pink Breast Cancer Awareness products—everything from clothing to kitchen appliances to M&M candies to tweezers. And consumers have bought them as a way to support a cause that is important to them.

In the next ten years, the trend toward purchasing with a purpose will continue to grow. Consumers will demand that the goods and services they purchase come from companies that are actively involved in doing good works in the community. We're at the forefront of this explosion of social consciousness and companies that haven't adopted a civic-minded business model will soon be left behind. In ten years, businesses won't have a choice if they want to be competitive—they can become socially conscious or shut down.

Still, some of you may be skeptical. We understand. We are constantly asked by our customers "How can you possibly donate your proceeds to charity and stay in business?" especially since we operate in a highly competitive industry with ever-shrinking profits.

We tell them, "We can't afford not to," which is the truth. The customer research we have conducted has told us quite clearly that the primary reason people buy from us is that we donate our proceeds to good works. They can buy the exact same ink and toner cartridges from hundreds of other companies, but we're the only retailer that takes their expenditure and reinvests it in good works.

But not only can such a model sustain a business, it can also yield higher profits. One reason for higher profitability is that you can keep prices just a little bit above market rates if you donate to good works. Consumers will pay a higher price if they know their money is going to a good cause.

Positioning your company as a socially conscious business is also useful when prospecting for new customers. Leading the conversation with information about the organizations your business supports, and the good works you do, makes the sales call much easier and the prospect much more receptive to your call.

A side benefit of running a socially conscious business is that customer loyalty is significantly higher and repeat business much more frequent than with typical for-profit companies.

Creating A Feel-Good Experience for Customers

Our goal with every customer contact is to make that customer feel appreciated, because they are, whether that contact comes through the Internet, phone, or mail. We are always looking for ways to improve our performance. So we decided to do a little experiment.

Recognizing that we have the most control over the quality of experience our phone customers have, we decided to test whether mentioning LaserMonks' good works had any impact on sales. For one week we split incoming calls into our call center. One of us answered the phone using our normal friendly phone technique, but did not make mention of our good works, and the other used the same telephone script with one difference: He or she reminded the customer that a portion of every dollar spent with us went to help those in need.

The results were very interesting. Customers who did not hear about our good works spent, on average, $60, while those who did spent $10 more per order. These people were also more likely to purchase extras such as monastery products, music, books, or coffee. Even on a more qualitative level, versus quantitative, these customers engaged the monkhelper more and generally seemed to be happier with their purchasing experience.

Although our week-long experiment was far from scientifically significant, it did reinforce the notion that it's okay to talk about good works—reminding customers will not negatively impact sales—and "cause marketing" is good for business.

▦ Finding a Charitable Fit

The most successful socially conscious businesses connect their products or services to related organizations. When you do that—create a linkage—it's much easier to weave the charitable giving aspect of your business into marketing and daily operations.

For example, LaserMonks recently added fresh-roasted, gourmet coffee to our product offerings. We did that so we could directly and indirectly help the farmers in the coffee-producing countries and offer a socially responsible product. We tell customers, "If you buy coffee from us, you are literally helping a poor farming family in Guatemala or Columbia or Africa." Every purchase generates demand for more product and allows us to funnel the proceeds of that sale back to the coffee growers. We now have a separate site, http://www.benevolentblends.com, specifically for the purchase of coffee. It details how we help sustain communities in coffee-growing regions.

Not only do customers enjoy drinking the gourmet coffee they buy from us, but knowing their purchase is making a difference makes them feel good.

We also like to donate based on the personality of LaserMonks. Because LaserMonks is a subsidiary of the abbey of Our Lady of Spring Bank, we make it a priority to help organizations related to the monastery, such as the Alliance for International Monasticism (AIM) or Place of Grace, a Catholic worker house in Wisconsin. These are the types of charities that best fit with LaserMonks, but similar matches can be found for virtually any type of business.

The important thing is to find the personality of your enterprise and to closely match it to the causes it supports, which should then be closely connected to the company's marketing strategy. For example, if you run a women's clothing store, you may prefer women-related causes, such as breast cancer awareness or domestic abuse. Or if you run a software development firm, educational nonprofits may be a good match. Or not. It all depends on what causes speak to you and your employees, and which also match how you're marketing—and to whom you're marketing—your products and services.

▦ Involve Your Customers in the Process

Once LaserMonks established its core business strategy and model of giving and put them into action, our next goal was to ramp up that level of giving. To take it to the next level, however, we needed the support of our workers and everyone who helped out at LaserMonks. They needed to understand the process and recognize the key role they play in attracting customers and bringing in more revenue, so we could support those less fortunate.

We also felt it was important to involve our customers in the giving process—to challenge them to conduct their business as we were conducting ours. So we started a program to educate our customers about our business model and encourage them to follow it. But we didn't jump right into this, we took it step-by-step:

- **Analysis.** First, we analyzed our customer base to see what types of organizations were buying from us, the number of employees, annual revenues, location, etc.

- **Start small.** We decided we would first roll out the program to our small business customers, who had more autonomy in decision making and could start small, like us.

- **Identify targets.** Next, we developed a list of customers we wanted to approach about participating, to see which ones might be interested.

- **Zero in.** Finally, we pared the list down through several rounds of communication with the small business owners we had initially identified.

The concept behind our new program was this: LaserMonks would donate a sum of money to the customer, which would be used to develop a charitable project with their employees. We didn't want them to simply turn around and give the money to a local charity but, rather, to use the money as start-up funds to initiate a bigger fundraiser that could have an even bigger impact. For example, the customer could use the seed money to host a spaghetti dinner to benefit the local soup kitchen. LaserMonks would fund the cost of the raw materials and the company would then aim to double or triple that gift through a specific money-making endeavor, like a spaghetti dinner.

To receive funds from us, participating customers were asked to prepare a document describing their initial plan for the donation. Once the project was completed, we asked for testimonials from employees describing how they felt working on the project and what they learned, either about their fellow employees, about the fundraising event, or the charity to which the money was donated. We also asked the company to get testimonials from the charity describing the impact of the company's donation.

This program is still in its infancy, but it's already striking a chord with small businesses we work with. We're looking forward to seeing what happens when major corporations accept the challenge!

▦ Bring Charity Down to the Individual Customer Level

Let's be honest, excitement and anticipation are two words you'll likely never hear associated with printer supplies. When a consumer walks into a national retail office supply chain to buy ink or toner, it is a very functional purchase—far from emotional. Ink and toner cartridges are pretty boring products and it's hard to get too attached to the process of paying for them.

But we're trying to change that process, and the (lack of) emotion associated with it, by involving customers in the giving process at LaserMonks. It's a challenge though, we readily admit.

When a person visits the LaserMonks Web site in search of the right ink or toner cartridge for their printer, we want to provide a product solution, but we also want to make them aware of the good they are doing by buying from us. It's a delicate balance—we don't want to distract them from their purchase, but we do want them to feel something when they buy from us, such as the satisfaction of knowing they're supporting good works.

To do that, we try to have Web site visitors immediately take note of our good works program. When a customer visits the LaserMonks Web site for the first time, they are usually very curious about us and our operation. In response, we try to provide plenty of information up front about the charities we support, including a "featured charity" on the front page. But we also want to remind them that we donate to their local community, or nonprofits in their area, as they move through the shopping process. We do this by sprinkling information about our giving on each page, so the customer's familiarity with us grows the longer they stay on the site.

Weaving charitable-giving information among product details is one way that we engage customers during their time shopping on the LaserMonks Web site. We differentiate the LaserMonks experience from the detached, unemotional buying experience at national chains. It's not overt, but more of a behind-the-scenes approach to linking a product purchase with the positive feeling one gets when performing a good deed.

Customers who contact us by phone also receive information about the charities we support. As we said earlier, we have anecdotal evidence that this improves sales, and makes our customers feel good. We've trained our call center operators to tell customers about the featured charities for that month and to ask if there is a certain organization that our customers would like to see us help. We want our customers to associate LaserMonks with giving, so that while they shop with us they receive the emotional benefit such good works provide.

▨ Surprise Customers by Giving On-the-Spot

Despite our attempt to be very open and honest about how we operate LaserMonks and how our charitable process works (it's pretty simple), it is surprising how skeptical some customers are. One case-in-point is a diocesan leader we spoke with recently.

We met him at a presentation to a Midwest Catholic diocese, where we talked about LaserMonks, our mission, and our products. We were there to show them how we could save them money on office products, which they routinely bought from the national office supply chains. But we also addressed how our mission of helping the needy meshed with the diocese's own mission.

The members of the audience—priests, teachers, and workers in the parish offices—listened politely, but there was little reaction to our pitch. They didn't seem to be getting our message.

We left, unsure of what else we could do or say to help them see our common goal. It turns out that we didn't have to do anything we wouldn't normally do.

About a week later we received a phone call from one of the audience members, an educational director at one of the schools in the diocese. He called to tell us about a family that had no money for school supplies for their five children.

Surprisingly, he was still skeptical, wondering if we really did what we said we did—give to those in need without question. "They could really use your help," he said, "but I don't expect you to help just based on a single phone call." What he did expect was to be refused.

We asked him to fax over a list of all the school supplies the family needed and checked to see if it would be okay if we shipped the supplies directly to the school for distribution to the family (we often prefer to donate anonymously). He said he would prepare a list, but still sounded wary.

The next day we received the fax from him and quickly mailed out a box of paper, notebooks, pencils, and crayons, as well as some things that were not on the list.

A week later we received an e-mail from him overflowing with praise and gratitude. He was tremendously thankful and couldn't believe that one phone call and fax could take care of this family's need.

Perhaps it was after hearing about the school supplies that other parishes made similar calls in the following weeks, asking if we could help other families in need. In all cases, we were happy to, not only because it is part of our mission and the relative cost is so low, but because giving is good business. These donations got our LaserMonks' foot in the door at many of the dioceses in that area, helping to establish new business relationships and generating significant sales.

▦ More Forgiving Customers

In addition to becoming loyal buyers, we've found that our customers, on the whole, are far more forgiving than your typical buyer. That is, customers frequently see the big picture and realize that one blunder on our part will not ruin their life. In fact, we often have customers apologizing to us when we make a mistake.

One situation stands out as an example of the level of forgiveness we've experienced with our customers.

Several years ago, during the start-up phase of LaserMonks, a small-business customer called to place his first order with us. We were thrilled and made every effort to wow him with our level of customer service. Unfortunately, we failed miserably.

First, we shipped him the wrong products.

When we discovered the error, we quickly sent out a package with the correct products. Sadly, we inadvertently mailed it to the wrong address.

So, again, we sent out a new shipment, with the proper products, to the correct address, only to have the customer report to us that one of the cartridges was leaking. We were horrified. Here we were, trying to impress this new customer, and all we felt was embarrassment at the comedy of errors.

What was most amazing, however, was the customer's reaction. We expected him to be outraged at the repeated goofs, to demand a refund, and to loudly exclaim that he would never, ever buy from us again. That's what we anticipated.

Instead, each time we spoke with him about the errors, he apologized to us and wanted to cover the cost of the additional shipments due to our mistakes. Throughout the ordeal he kept telling us how happy he was to be purchasing from an organization that cared about the community. He was very aware of the fact that the proceeds were going to help others and didn't want to take money away from those projects. Nevertheless, we insisted on assuming the additional costs due to our own mistakes.

Businesses are not perfect and LaserMonks and its helpers make just as many errors as other companies. But because of our socially conscious message, rarely do we have a customer who is negative or difficult to deal with, even when we are at fault.

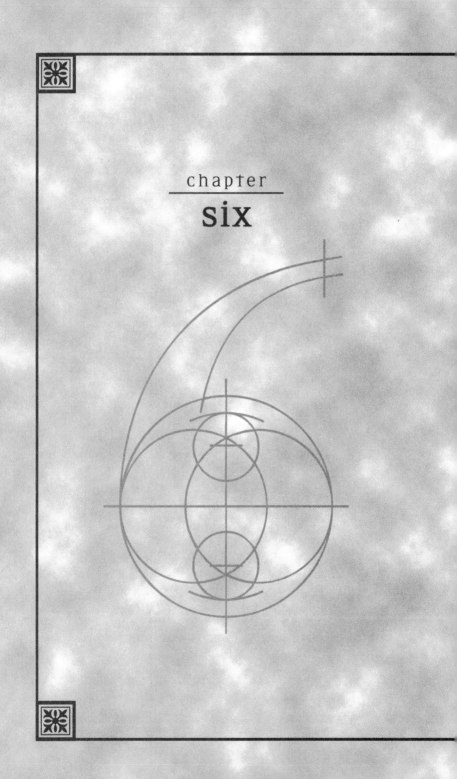

chapter
six

creating
a successful
e-business

ONE OF THE MANY ADVANTAGES OF RUNNING
AN E-COMMERCE BUSINESS IS ITS GLOBAL REACH.
NOT ONLY CAN YOU SERVE CUSTOMERS IN YOUR
COMMUNITY, BUT THOSE HALFWAY AROUND THE
WORLD, JUST AS EASILY.

WE WERE REMINDED OF THIS NOT TOO LONG
AGO WHILE TALKING WITH OUR PROGRAMMER,
AN INDEPENDENT CONTRACTOR WHO HAPPENS TO
LIVE IN THE UNITED KINGDOM. HE TOLD US THAT

during a recent conversation with his Web-hosting company about some technical issues, his contact mentioned having just returned from a companywide training session, where they heard about a unique company called LaserMonks. Apparently, Laser-Monks, a small business in Wisconsin, was a case study in superior customer service thousands of miles away in the United Kingdom. Who knew we were so well-known?!

Despite the fact that some companies are now positioning us as experts in running a successful e-commerce business, we want to make it clear that there are many ways to build an e-commerce venture. Depending on your products and services, the demographics of your customer base, your channels of distribution—online, mail order, brick-and-mortar, telemarketing, etc.—you might build an entirely different business model than ours. What we did has worked very well, but it's not the only way to go.

That being said, there are lessons we learned and experiences we had that certainly shaped how LaserMonks operates.

▒ Drop Ship or Sink

One of our first lessons was that drop-shipping would be our distribution model. Drop-shippers are wholesalers willing to ship their products—which they either purchase or manufacture in huge quantities—directly to your customers under your brand. "Blind" drop-shipping, which we use, allows a business like LaserMonks to run online only without a brick-and-mortar location, as the vendor ships customer orders directly from their warehouse.

Today drop-shipping is critical for us because it enables us to serve thousands of customers at a time without personally having to physically handle each individual shipment. We carefully evaluated and tested each drop-ship provider before entrusting them with our valuable customer shipments. But when we were just starting out, drop-shipping was important for others reasons, as well.

As a near-startup business when we, MonkHelper Marketing, Inc., became involved, LaserMonks didn't have a lot of cash to reinvest in the business. Using a drop-shipper meant that LaserMonks didn't have to invest significantly in inventory, and we didn't have to spend time every day packaging up customer orders. We could take advantage of the drop shipper's high-volume lower shipping rates and use their product images rather than paying to take our own. We could keep our overall financial risk down because we received payment up front for customer purchases before we had to pay the shipper.

Many companies in the ink and toner business use the drop ship model for all the reasons we have just outlined. Why assume the risk of manufacturing, storing, managing, and shipping products when you can economically turn over that responsibility to a specialist to handle.

Because drop-shippers manufacture and ship in such huge quantities, they are often able to negotiate extremely reasonable shipping rates. A few that we work with are willing to pass along those tremendous savings—around 40 percent lower than we could obtain. But not all are as generous. Just because a drop-shipper can get an advantageous shipping rate does not necessarily mean that you will benefit from it. Be sure to ask.

▦ In Search Of…

So how do you find a reputable, trustworthy drop-shipper? We started by asking other Web site owners what companies they used, and we did a lot of research using industry magazines as our guide, since that is where most drop-shippers advertise. And then we contacted them. Repeatedly.

As we examined their capabilities, we also looked at their client lists in the hopes of seeing names of companies we recognized, or companies with a similar customer demographic—a mix of corporate, small office/home office (SOHO), mid-sized businesses, and individual users.

After gathering information about their services, their product quality and pricing, we asked them to prove themselves. That meant running drop-ship tests with them to see how they performed, and talking with current customers that were approximately our size, to confirm that the drop-shipper worked just as hard for a growing small business as it did for a major client. We watched each potential drop-shipper very closely to note any potential problems. Our thoroughness ended up saving us several times when less reputable drop-shippers didn't hold up their end of the bargain.

One company we decided to try was a supplier to a very large and well-known Web site, so we assumed they would do a good job. Things started off well, but midway through our test with them, we began to see a very high defect rate in their products. Customers were calling with complaints about their shipment's quality. We couldn't imagine why until we investigated and discovered that the drop-shipper had, unbeknownst to us, switched the product. Instead of sending the one we had specified, the drop-shipper was mailing out an inferior one.

Hundreds of our customers had received this poor quality product. Once we realized what had happened, we replaced each and every bad cartridge at our cost. We tried to turn a disaster caused by the drop-shipper into a positive experience for the customer, but it was a challenge—one we didn't expect. But because we were watching the drop-shipper so closely, and staying in close contact with customers, we were alerted about the problem shortly after it occurred. Needless to say, we stopped doing business with the drop-shipper immediately. Be aware that with every shipment, you are putting your company's reputation in the drop-shipper's hands. Some are worthy of that trust and some are not.

Another factor we consider is the locations of the drop-shipper's multiple warehouses and whether they complement our customer hubs. We also look at how well the warehouses are stocked with products our customers regularly buy, as well as the drop-shipper's ability to ship "non-stock" items for us.

If you read between the lines of some of these requirements, you'll see that flexibility is important. We need drop-shippers that can adapt to our company's evolving needs and requests, including the ability and willingness to add items to the shipments from time-to-time. When we first started carrying Trappistine Creamy Caramels, for instance, we wanted to place samples in each customer order. Our biggest vendor refused to make any additions to the boxes they shipped, but our other vendor was very flexible and had no problem adding that additional step. That helped not just when we wanted to send along product samples, but continues to be helpful whenever we want to pass along a special promotional offer or coupon. Without flexibility on the part of the drop-shipper, you can miss out on terrific, low-cost marketing opportunities.

But flexibility applies to pricing, as well. When remanufactured cartridges experience an industry-wide price drop, we expect the vendor to pass along that lower price to us, just as they pass along the inevitable increases.

We've also tried to be flexible regarding data interchange technology, which enables e-commerce sites to talk to each other without human intervention. This allows dealer and fulfillment center computers to talk regularly and update each other regarding shipments to be sent, inventory requirements, payments, and more. For us, it's an important piece of the e-commerce puzzle and we ask that our vendors use it, or that they are at least headed toward using it in the near future, in order to reduce the amount of non-automated (read: time-consuming) communication that has to occur.

Although not all vendors are willing to jump on the data interchange technology bandwagon just because we need them to, some are. In fact, one of our vendors, a very high-quality provider of remanufactured ink cartridges, went so far as to adopt data interchange technology specifically for us. We aren't the company's largest customer by far, but they worked with us to make it happen because they recognized the value it brought to our operations. That willingness to be helpful and flexible—is one of the many reasons we continue to do business with this organization year after year.

All of this brings up the issue of corporate personality. To be successful, your company needs to be in sync with your vendors. Personality is certainly subjective, but you need your fulfillment center—the vendor who will have direct contact with *your* customers—to virtually mirror your company's operational policies and customer mandates.

Finally, we look for companies where there is long-term growth potential. As LaserMonks grows, we want to feel confident that our drop-shippers will grow with us, keeping pace or outpacing us. Companies that are wedded to outdated technology or processes, or seem uninterested in their own growth are not good candidates for us.

▦ Customer Care Is at the Core

Drop-shipping is a critical competency in e-commerce, for obvious technological reasons. Perhaps not so obvious, however, is that customer service—what we like to call customer hospitality—is equally important. Since you have so few ways to connect with the customer online—you don't meet them in person and in many instances you don't speak to them— your Web site and response to customer inquiries defines how your online business is perceived. Will your customers have a pleasant experience? Will it be heartwarming? Efficient? Curt? Time-consuming? Frustrating? Maddening? Or perfect?

Each customer's experience at your company's Web site determines how likely he or she will visit and buy from you again. Each negative experience diminishes the customer's lifetime value and potential for referrals, reducing the company's total future revenues. In plain language, if your customers have a bad experience, they probably won't buy from you again and instead of raving about your products and services to others, they'll complain, thus dissuading others from buying, as well. It's a slippery slope you don't want to navigate.

To avoid any negative experiences, the solution is to focus heavily on customer care and those responsible for providing it.

LaserMonks invests heavily in training and skill building so that our core mission resonates with each person or business partner who has a relationship with us. That is, we provide on-the-job training to help them perform above expectations at their particular tasks, but we also bring in outside training companies or go off-site for training on bigger issues.

In addition to training in how to operate the equipment needed to run the business, such as the telephone, Web site, and office equipment, we provide instruction in all types of written communication; verbal, written, and online. Since communication with customers can make or break an experience with LaserMonks, we recognized its importance from day one. But we don't simply work on how to speak in complete, grammatically correct sentences. We also help our workers convey how pleased and appreciative we are that our customers have chosen to buy from us. Customers have so many other options that we want to stand out in their minds. We also want to communicate warmth and friendliness in our communication, a skill that can be challenging to teach. Our goal is for each customer to feel that we are speaking directly to him or her in our e-mails or phone calls. We do not want our communication to feel impersonal and mass-generated.

Our ability to teach these skills is determined, in part, by how well we choose the people who work with LaserMonks. In pursuing partnerships, we look at how well they mesh with the personality of our organization, and how well we expect they will get along with our current core team. That means assessing the types of personalities we have in-house and choosing new personalities that will jibe with those.

Matching worker skills with tasks is another aspect of choosing excellent customer care helpers. We don't assume that everyone is qualified to perform every task; rather, we choose those with specific abilities and preferences and assign them projects or tasks that match their skills. In doing this, we increase the odds that they will thrive in their assignments and enjoy their work. From there, we keep an eye out for other jobs that suit their personality and experiences.

Workers have a proven ability to learn and adapt, so we don't try to pigeonhole them into one job description forever. But we do try to fashion jobs that will make the most of their interests and abilities, so that both workers and customers will be happy with their experience at LaserMonks.

Managing the process has proven challenging at times, but by making a positive customer experience our first priority, many other issues resolve themselves. When questions arise about how to handle a customer complaint, or how to rectify a problem a customer is having, we remind ourselves of The Rule, and do whatever is needed to please the customer. That may mean overnighting a replacement cartridge, refunding a customer's purchase price, or simply listening. When we do hear complaints from customers, it usually has little to do with their actual order and more to do with how they've been treated. We work hard to turn their attitude around and give them a bright spot in their day.

We've learned that experience in customer service is less important than basic personality traits like honesty, friendliness, a pleasant phone voice, a willingness to learn and, most important, a commitment to convey our message to customers. Over time, we have shifted our perception of the perfect Monk-Helper. Through The Rule of St. Benedict, we realized that instead of projecting what we need onto a worker in the hopes of finding a match, we need to listen to what the person has to offer and match that with what we need. Sometimes that may require creating a job description different from what we had been looking for. But in the end, we find people who are eager to work, eager to apply their talents, and eager to learn more about LaserMonks and how they can help.

Relying on the local workforce in our working class community has been important for us, not only because we feel strongly about helping our neighbors, but because our workers need to be on-site. This way they can meet the monks and experience the monastery firsthand, both essential components in doing the best job possible for LaserMonks. They are given a tour of the abbey, see the monks' lifestyle, are invited to attend mass, and are encouraged to take walks on the property during breaks or after work. That close connection to the monastery helps the workers get a feeling for what LaserMonks is all about, and helps them communicate that specialness to our customers. We feel strongly that without that firsthand interaction, workers would be much less effective at conveying our message and our corporate personality.

Just as we assign workers jobs that are appropriate for their skill sets, we use technology that is appropriate for our current and future e-commerce needs. We do everything economically, as most successful small businesses do, but we're not afraid to invest money in infrastructure that will serve us well for years.

▦ E-commerce Technology Tutorial

Although our e-commerce system is very robust now, that wasn't the case when we were just getting started. We started with the very small, basic, and inflexible e-commerce technology Father Bernard developed with the help of a programmer in Australia. This system proved challenging to use. It worked fine when the volume was five orders a day, but as the business began to grow, we encountered some difficulties. One was communication—the programmer operated in a time zone that was virtually the opposite of ours and spoke English with some difficulty. We could deal with that, but because the software was custom-written, we had to have the original programmer take care of each and every new feature addition. We had no other options initially and had to meet their financial demands to make any modifications.

Within a year, however, we were able to research, plan, design, and transfer our business to a new, modular e-commerce platform. We created both short- and long-term technology plans, mapping out features we believed the site needed immediately and those we wanted to migrate to over the next two to three years. Specifically, our plans detailed our goals, milestones, tasks, resources, budgets, and projections, and incorporated Gantt and PERT charts. We approached our technology needs in a modular fashion, taking each basic building block separately and then bringing the whole together into a functional system. It is how we've always done things: Start with the detailed customer requirements, figure out how to translate that into functional technology, and then merge it with the existing system. We don't try to address every technological issue at once or we'd never have an operational site.

We are fortunate that Cindy's expertise is Web design, enabling her to single-handedly rebuild the site, bit by bit. Not only is the site more flexible and robust, but it cost us far less to rebuild it from scratch than it would have to continue working with the old programmer and site.

The main components of our e-commerce technology platform have always been:

- Web site design
- E-commerce platform
- Order fulfillment
- Back-office/administration/accounting platform
- Robust Web site analytics
- Security
- Order management
- Payment processing

- Web site performance
- Hosting/server
- Customer feedback

We have always kept a journal of potential revisions, customer comments, and problems with the site. Anytime an idea or observation comes up, we note it in the journal. Then, we upgrade the system based on those notes each quarter. We tackle a major overhaul once a year. In fact, we're always in planning, scheduling, revising, or upgrading mode. Keeping track of who's doing what when is key to our getting anything done.

Keeping abreast of new technologies is critical for effectively addressing customer requests and suggestions regarding an e-commerce site. To stay ahead of the curve in terms of information, we religiously read and keep as reference material many technology guides, as well as industry magazines on technology, e-retailing, multi-channel marketing, and other business publications.

We also attend industry trade shows in the hopes of catching a glimpse of the next generation of e-commerce technology. Some of the popular trade shows are helpful, but they also tend to be very hard sell and you can easily become convinced that you need expensive services when you really don't. We've learned to stay far away from consultants who promise they can immediately increase Web site revenue or traffic. Many small business owners have been separated from tens of thousands of dollars when they didn't really need the additional services the consultants were pushing, or when the services they paid for didn't achieve the desired results.

In many cases, we have found that following our instincts is a smart strategy. A few years ago, we had a consulting firm try to convince us that we needed to put a customer satisfaction survey on the site, at the end of the checkout process. While we are all for customer satisfaction, we weren't convinced asking our customers to complete such a survey was a smart move. Our resistance to the idea led the consultants to suggest that we didn't really know what we were doing.

Instead of becoming adversarial, we took a more monastic approach. We took a poll of a subset of customers, asking them how they would react to a post-sale satisfaction survey. Sixty percent of those we polled said they would be "Very annoyed" and of those, 25 percent would be "Angry." This proved to us that they did not want a satisfaction survey at the site and confirmed that we really did know what we were doing, despite the consultants' opinion.

However, we are also willing to grow and keep up with technology and trends. With the advent of Web 2.0, we now realize that there are many ways to gather customer feedback. The next version of our Web site will include these features.

Just as we look to industry experts at trade shows for guidance in what's coming next, we also look to other companies in our industry as role models. We do not perceive them as competitors and many have been more than happy to share information about their e-commerce experiences.

To start your own study of companies in your marketplace, we recommend you first Google keywords that customers use to find you, in order to identify the top Web sites. Then carefully evaluate each and every site, really spend time there to get a sense of the company's strengths, weaknesses, and personality. Also, place an order at the site to experience firsthand what *their* customers' experience. Finally, call or e-mail the owner of the site or someone in customer service and be up front about your identity and information needs. Ask questions and engage in a dialogue in which you share information about your company, too. The worst that can happen is that the companies will tell you they won't share information, and that's really not so terrible. The upside is that you may gain extremely helpful suggestions and insights from those willing to speak with you, as we often have.

Of course, one issue to keep top-of-mind as you're studying similar e-commerce sites is how you want your business to be perceived relative to the major players, i.e., the "big boys." On one hand, a site that mimics the look and feel of a larger company in the same industry can provide credibility by association. However, your brand may become overshadowed in the presence of a big player, and a better solution may be to clearly differentiate your business. We try to straddle that dichotomy by designing our site to look well-established and corporate, while emphasizing our unique message and mission. Other companies just can't compete with us on that score.

Asking questions is always a good policy, especially as it applies to your vendors and suppliers. What dos and don'ts would they offer, based on having watched other e-commerce sites come on the market and then fold. What are the smartest moves they've seen their clients make? And what missteps have surely caused the downfall of others? What trends or forecasts do they predict? Vendors are in the unique position of being able to watch the market as a whole and should be capable of commenting on the moves and approaches some of the players have made.

Another group you want to question is your customer base. Find out who they are, why they buy from you, what they like most and least about your products and your Web site, and what it would take to get them to buy more. Study their purchasing patterns and abandonment rates to determine who comes to the site and leaves without buying. Being able to attack that statistic—converting visitors into buyers—can significantly impact your company's bottom line. But the key question to answer is why they don't buy.

Actually implementing suggested changes will require the services of programmers who can be contractors or staff members. Deciding whether you want programmers in-house or whether you prefer to outsource that work is a pivotal decision that needs to be made early on in your e-commerce business development.

Back when we were building our e-commerce platform virtually from scratch, we turned to an online forum for the open source software we used. Open source means that it is free, first of all, and that the source code for the program is available to anyone to modify it. Our platform is called ZenCart™, and is an evolution of Oscommerce™, another well-known platform. Before committing to it, we spent more than a year researching dozens of e-commerce platforms of all types, prices, and features.

One of the major pluses of this platform was that at the time there was a small, tight-knit group of loyal followers who were very helpful. Additionally, the canned package we started with had many built-in features we needed, so we didn't have to totally revamp what we had already built.

Open code worked well for us early on, but before you go jumping on the bandwagon you need to be aware that the coders who make upgrades are often volunteers who do so because they are dedicated to the product. Consequently, the software is not always stable or stealthy, there are no scheduled upgrades, and there are possible security issues because the coders are working on their own dime. You could potentially spend more money on the open source code in the long run, hiring a programmer only to find he or she overpromised and underdelivered. We were fortunate, in that the programmer we hired is fantastic and has been able to develop custom modules for LaserMonks using the open source code. LaserMonks has even become somewhat of a model site for the platform, according to the coders. In fact, ZenCart™

has become so popular on its own that we have dozens of other Web sites interested in buying the add-on modules we developed. To meet that need without giving away the store, soon we will be making those modules available for sale through a new Web site, at www.totallyzennedout.com.

Canned software, by comparison, is usually more established, offers the ability to lease the system, provides more up-front features, stability, good training guides and videos, and includes planned upgrades to the system. In general, canned systems are more robust. Then again, they are very costly, less flexible, and offer less potential for new features.

Budgeting is another aspect of the equation to keep in mind as you weigh the open source/canned platform options. How much do you have to invest in a functional e-commerce system? How much do you have budgeted for upgrades? Those questions alone may determine whether you are in a position to opt for a canned program. Creating and staying within a budget will help ensure you are still in business in a couple of years, since technology costs have been known to spiral out of control.

Once you have your platform in place and begin working on the look and feel of your e-commerce engine, i.e., your Web site, pay close attention to the content versus e-commerce balance. The customer's shopping experience is the most important aspect of your site. They want the ability to order quickly and easily. But if they have questions or need reassurance that yours is a legitimate business, you need to have enough content to help them. That means incorporating an "About Us" page that tells your story, a "FAQs" page, and any other resources you believe would be of value to your customers. That might include usage tips, troubleshooting charts, or links to organizations they may be interested in. You want to provide enough content to make your customer's shopping experience pleasant and stress-free, but you also want to build in reasons for them to come back. Frequently that means adding useful content they can't find elsewhere.

With your e-commerce site operational and customers placing orders, your next concern should be security. Actually, security should be a concern from the get-go, since hackers can wreak havoc on your business if customers find their credit card information has been stolen.

We use a contract security/site monitoring specialist to constantly keep watch over our site. For a monthly fee, this company helps keep our site and our customers secure. Because of the trust we place in them, starting with giving them access to the inner workings of our site, we spent quite a bit of time researching security companies. We asked colleagues and other Web site owners whom they used; then we did our own due diligence to be sure we felt comfortable handing over our pride and joy. Although the monitoring service is a type of insurance for us, we also make use of regular system backups and firewalls for basic protection. You should, too.

▦ Getting Customers in the Door

A successful e-commerce business requires customers, lots of them. But building a Web site does not mean they will find it on their own. You need to invest time and money in marketing your site to your target audience. LaserMonks has managed to do that without spending a lot of money, although our techniques are not necessarily unique. What is unique is our message, which is why many of these marketing methods work well for us.

Because LaserMonks is a small business, we don't have a lot of money to spend on anything, including marketing. In the beginning, when we literally had no money, that meant we were limited to free marketing tactics. These work well and we continue to use them today, although we now have a little money to spend, too.

The best free marketing methods are: media exposure, success stories you can share, and customer communication.

Media exposure, or publicity, is the fastest and cheapest way to get new customers. By issuing a press release to the media your target audience pays attention to, you can get the word out about your business to thousands or tens of thousands of people without paying a cent. It does require time, however. To pursue publicity effectively you need to have something newsworthy to report, such as a new product, helpful feature, an award your business has won, or something philanthropic you've been involved with. You can e-mail the release, but it should be written in a newsy—not self-promotional—style of writing. Once you've distributed the release to the media, they take it from there, potentially including the information in an upcoming issue or broadcast. When that happens, prepare to see your Web site visits dramatically increase.

In March 2003, a writer from a Minneapolis/ St. Paul newspaper, the *St. Paul Pioneer Press*, wrote what would turn out to be the catalyst for the media's interest in LaserMonks. The story got picked up by the Associated Press (AP) and was subsequently picked up by most of the major newspapers in the United States and a few internationally. (This story also was the first to coin the phrase "monk e-business," which would be used many other times by the media over the next few years.)

Of the many newspaper, television, and radio stories that have been done on LaserMonks, I think this story really resonated with us and with readers because of the writer's passion and understanding of our mission. And after seeing the impact such publicity could have on our business, we continue to pursue media exposure whenever we can.

With the publication of this article, the two of us were hard-pressed to answer the hundreds of phone calls daily, and literally thousands of e-mail inquiries we received as a result. Our orders at that time were somewhere between 50 to 100 per day, and for the few weeks after the article came out, orders skyrocketed to more than 300 per day. Because of the nature of the AP, our story was picked up by various newspapers across the United States, and over the next several months we saw a ripple effect. The daily orders settled in at 100 to 150 per day, after the initial publication, but we would see a rise and fall when it was published in a new market. For the most part, this rise was the only way we were aware that more media attention had been bestowed upon LaserMonks. Customers would call from all over the country, and comment on our news story, which ran in papers from Miami, Florida to Anchorage, Alaska, and every large market in between.

Another effective marketing tool is testimonials, or customer success stories. People love reading about how others benefit from doing business with you. You can either sprinkle them throughout the site or have a specific spot where you feature a list of customer comments and raves, followed by their real name. The name is needed for authenticity—initials just don't cut it for the skeptics.

Testimonials can be time-consuming to gather, especially when you're relying on the customers to provide them. One way we speed up that process is by offering to draft something for the customer to approve based on what they tell us they love about LaserMonks. We also try and capture different customer stories, rather than hitting hard on any one element of the business. For example, we enjoy stories from customers who have witnessed the good works we have done and how others benefited, but we also welcome comments about interactions with our customer care workers, how easy it is to find the products they need, how much money they saved, or something else. Testimonials provide credibility by allowing your customers to help sell your products and services.

The third top marketing tool, in addition to publicity and testimonials, is customer communication, which generally costs absolutely nothing, especially when the customer reaches out to you. Each e-mail that is sent, each information request that is received, phone call that comes in, or note that accompanies an order is a marketing opportunity that few businesses recognize. We take this so seriously that we do regular training with our MonkHelpers so they can see how everything they say, write, and communicate to customers or potential customers affects LaserMonks.

Unlike other e-commerce businesses that focus on attracting new customers to the fold, we concentrate on customer retention. By working hard to satisfy current customers and give them reasons to buy from us again, they become our second-best source of new customer referrals—satisfied customers tell their friends, families, coworkers, churches, you name it. Not only does keeping our current customers happy reduce our marketing expenses, it also boosts our corporate reputation, which can lead back to media exposure, testimonials, and positive customer communication. At press time, LaserMonks had recently employed other, more viral techniques such as forums and blogs to monitor customer comments.

To keep track of all our marketing activities, we use a marketing plan. It helps us identify coming opportunities we need to prepare for, as well as making it clear when we need to initiate a new marketing initiative.

▨ LaserMonks Marketing Plan

EXECUTIVE OVERVIEW AND SUMMARY: *This defines who LaserMonks is and what makes us unique*

- **MARKETING OBJECTIVES**

  1. Target Markets—corporate customers, SOHO, individual consumers, etc.
  2. Product Profile—describes our product

- **MARKET RESEARCH AND ANALYSIS**

  1. Analysis of Target Market Marketshare—We did a study of our industry and the percentages of each group and how much they were spending and projecting growth over 10 years. (Laser-Monks subscribes to several research services.)
  2. Analysis of Our Current Situation—We update this every quarter describing where we currently are and where we want to be.
  3. Target Market Growth—How much will the ink and toner market grow? How will the demographics change and grow?
  4. Market Needs and Trends

- **PRODUCT ANALYSIS**

  1. Product Profile
  2. Product Distribution—We decided early on to go with the drop-ship method.

Marketing Strategy

1. What are LaserMonks' main strategies?
2. LaserMonks' Mission
3. Marketing Objectives
4. Financial Objectives
5. Marketing Budget

Marketing Methods

1. Media
2. E-mail
3. Web site
4. Direct Marketing
5. Non-Internet Advertising
6. Internet Advertising
7. Natural Search Selection
8. Telephone Marketing

- **WEB SITE ANALYTICS**

  1. Demographics
  2. Exit pages
  3. Conversions

Marketing Budgets, Projection and Forecasts

Marketing Milestones

Keys to Success

1. Critical Issues

2. LaserMonks' Strengths—our customer care and hospitality and our mission

3. LaserMonks' Weaknesses—very competitive industry with shrinking margins

4. Market Opportunities—growing population of Internet users

5. Industry Environment

Keeping your marketing budget under control is a challenge at times, especially when you are presented with so many wonderful opportunities to get the word out about your online business. However, being able to refer to your plan and your budget does make such decisions easier. If the money hasn't been allocated for a major spread in a national magazine, it simply can't happen this year. Do not go over budget in order to try out a new tool you haven't fully investigated and considered previously. Rarely do such spur-of-the-moment opportunities turn out to be better than what you had already planned.

Having a clearly delineated plan also helps us evaluate the return on investment (ROI) of each marketing campaign. We can more easily track what we did and what kind of results we obtained. That way we can compare our campaigns moving forward and do more of what worked and less of what didn't.

That's not to say we don't experiment with new marketing methods, we do. But we don't invest a significant portion of our budget on an untested concept. We first see how it performs. You may find a tool that costs less than something you're already doing, but the payoff is only a fraction more. Or you could discover a tactic that costs more, but gets better results, making it worth the additional cash outlay. Keep in mind that your competitors are routinely testing new marketing methods, and so should you.

We are just beginning to use paid search, for example. It's a mysterious process with data that is hard to analyze, unlike e-mail marketing, which we've been doing for years. We've had major success with e-mail marketing, where we mine our existing data and create e-mail campaigns based on that information. We do all the design in-house and then use a major e-mail marketing service to send and track each campaign. We routinely watch the percent of opens, click-throughs, and conversions to orders, and we try new approaches to better the results of each mailing. We have trained our customers to expect e-mails from us, and it works.

But in case our customers become bored with e-mails, we want to stay ahead of the pack marketing-wise, which is why we are always on the lookout for the next great online marketing tool (such as online videos and blogs).

Running a successful e-commerce business is a blend of managing customer care workers, using appropriate Internet technology, and enticing customers to the Web site through marketing.

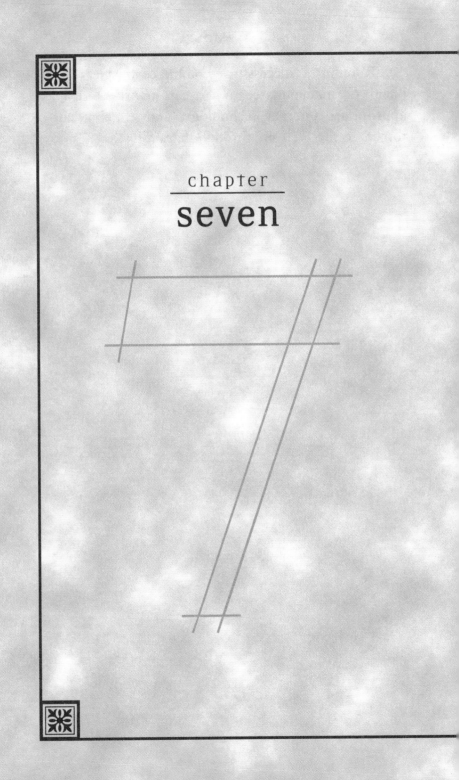

chapter
seven

creating
a market space

THE INK AND TONER MARKETPLACE TODAY IS SIMILAR IN MANY WAYS TO THE INDUSTRY IN 2002, WHEN LASERMONKS WAS FOUNDED. NOW, FIVE YEARS LATER, IT IS STILL HUGE, AT $12.6 BILLION IN SIZE; GROWING AT A RATE OF MORE THAN 7 PERCENT ANNUALLY[1]; AND HAS MANY PLAYERS OF ALL SIZES, FROM NATIONAL OFFICE

---

[1] Source: Freedonia.com, April 2007

supply chains to mom-and-pop retailers. But its size and complexity didn't deter Father Bernard from wanting to carve out a unique niche within the crowded market. In fact, he found an underserved customer base and aimed to create a new market space.

Customers for ink and toner cartridges range from individuals with home computers and printers, to home office users, small businesses, nonprofits, government agencies, educational and religious institutions, and major corporations; in essence, everyone who owns a printer, copier, or fax machine.

For many years, customers who only bought occasionally or in smaller quantities typically headed to an office supply retailer for their ink and toner. Larger organizations, on the other hand, ordered in bulk through purchase orders or blanket contracts either with national sellers or wholesalers, negotiating better pricing than the little guys.

Well, Father Bernard and the monks of Our Lady of Spring Bank were one of the little guys, paying what they felt were exorbitant fees for printer supplies. While the cost for smaller printers has dropped precipitously, the cost of the ink cartridges has risen dramatically and is now seven times more expensive than vintage champagne, says *The Internet Retailer's* Top 500 report. Increasingly, buyers headed online for more competitive pricing. In 2006, ink and toner buyers spent $10.3 billion online in 2006, according to *The Internet Retailer's* Top 500. However, even online, the big box retailers still dominate: Office Depot is number one in this category.

Another strategy smaller companies and individuals adopted in an effort to reduce their ink expenses was refilling cartridges, rather than buying new each time they needed more ink. Kits for refilling cartridges manually proliferated, as well as franchised refill stores. Then the larger chain stores entered the refill market, as well as the less expensive compatible category, in an effort to win back customers defecting to other sources for their ink and toner.

▓ The Changing Aftermarket Cartridge Industry

In the last five years, there have been a number of changes within the aftermarket cartridge industry—that is, the market for remanufactured inkjet cartridges.

First, the development and marketing of lower-cost color laser printers is causing people to make the switch from traditional black-and-white to full color printing. From single-use color printers to multi-function printer/copier/scanner units, color will in the next 10 years, dominate and change the landscape for ink and toner cartridges, too.

Along with the increased use of color in printing, and the increasing demand for color ink products, came rising competition among sellers. In order to compete, retailers and e-tailers began dropping their prices, thereby lowering profit margins on brand name ink and toner cartridges.

At about the same time, consumers fed up with the high cost of ink and toner began looking into less expensive alternatives, such as remanufactured products, compatible cartridges, and refilling. The prices on these were much less than the brand name offerings—so much less that many consumers decided to try them out.

Recognizing the shift in consumer purchasing, major retail office supply chains began selling compatible and remanufactured ink and toner cartridges to meet growing demand. Although at first the quality was inconsistent, over time the quality of the lower-cost alternatives improved.

Within the last five years, concern about the environment has also significantly increased, driving more consumers to investigate ways to recycle or refill cartridges. The popularity of remanufactured cartridges has risen as a result.

To be responsive to its customers, LaserMonks has closely followed, and in some cases led, these market shifts, beginning by carrying compatible and remanufactured cartridges years ago, and more recently, with the launch of its aggressive recycling program.

As the demand for ink and toner cartridges shifted from black to color, and interest in lower-cost alternatives rose, LaserMonks competitors converged into three main categories:

- Online-only e-tailers
- Retail chain stores
- Refill stores

Online-only businesses typically sell compatible and remanufactured cartridges at very low prices, due to lower overhead costs than brick-and-mortar retailers. Some observers might argue that these ventures are in direct competition with LaserMonks, but we take the position that we have no direct competition because no other ink and toner company gives all its proceeds to charity. That's what differentiates us—more than our pricing, marketing, or customer service.

Retail chain stores are the well-known brick-and-mortar operations that typically also have supplementary online channels. Refill stores are the newest channel and allow customers to bring in their empty cartridges to be refilled.

▣ Looking at a Familiar Market from a Different Perspective

Most companies focus on matching and beating their competition, using many of the same strategies to try to woo customers. Of course, when all is said and done, the only real distinguishing characteristics are minor improvements in cost or quality—nothing revolutionary or memorable. Recognizing the difficulty of setting ourselves apart from already established ink and toner sellers, we decided to think differently about our industry and what we had to offer.

Many online ink and toner sites must compete on price to attract new customers and keep the ones they have. They must also convince potential customers of the cost advantages of remanufactured or compatible cartridges versus the brand name leaders. With such an emphasis on price, we didn't see much opportunity to build long-term relationships with our customers— with low prices as their first priority, any week that we weren't the low-cost provider would be the week they did business with someone else. That didn't seem to be a winning business model for LaserMonks.

We decided early in the process to offer customers a choice each time they visited the Web site: They could purchase the brand name, well-known cartridges that have a reputation for reliability, or save some money by using cost saving, alternative cartridges that we also carry. We closely aligned Laser-Monks with *both* the brand name manufacturers and the remanufacturing industry, thereby bridging the gap between online retailers and the big box stores.

By offering a choice, we earned the credibility of carrying brand name products, but also the attractiveness of potential cost savings remanufactured and compatible products can provide.

If a customer wanted to save money, we could offer remanufactured or compatible products at very competitive pricing and with quality assurances and guarantees (as well as the word of the monks). But, if a customer was resistant to non–brand name cartridges, despite the possible savings, we could offer the names they were familiar with and not lose the sale. And either way, prospects and customers knew the money went to helping the less fortunate, which was a reason to buy from us no matter what their product preference.

▦ Introducing a New Value Proposition

Early on, we asked ourselves why customers would purchase from us over other Internet sites, or from us instead of the well-known retail chain stores. In other words, what new value proposition could we introduce to a basic product?

As we brainstormed, we posed these questions:

- What factors could LaserMonks create that the ink and toner industry has never offered?

- What factors could Lasermonks eliminate in the ink and toner industry?

- What factors could LaserMonks raise above the industry standard?

Here's what we came up with:

- We could work to build a trust in our cost-saving, alternative cartridges because of who we were (and because other industry participants had not made an effort to do so).

- We could eliminate the distrust that many consumers have when considering whether to buy remanufactured or compatible ink and toner versus the brand name by guaranteeing their performance or offering to replace them.

- We could go well beyond the industry standards of philanthropy by dedicating all of

the company's profits to charitable works—
not just some of the proceeds, but all of them.

Those goals provided a path for our marketing to follow that would differentiate LaserMonks from all the other companies out there selling what we were selling.

▦ We Don't Have Competition

Unlike other companies in the ink and toner industry, LaserMonks has always approached other companies as allies, not competitors. Perhaps because we sell remanufactured products, which are the underdog product, our feeling is that sellers of these products must stick together against the Goliaths of the brand name category. By sharing information among ourselves, those companies selling remanufactured and compatible ink and toner cartridges can help educate our customer base about the benefits of such products and, together, increase the overall size of the market. In doing so, we increase sales for everyone, not just LaserMonks.

We are also always willing to share information about our business because, ultimately, we want other companies—even those in our industry—to follow our lead and business model. We have never considered the big chain stores our competition either, because our mission and goals are totally divergent. However, big chain stores are solidly established and will always have a very large share of the market, if only because at times it is simply more convenient to drive down the street to Big Box Store A than to order online. And we have never discouraged customers from using this convenience.

We have learned so much from the established retail stores—we have studied how they run their businesses and have taken their weaknesses and made sure those weaknesses are our strengths, on top of other strengths, of course. But we don't consider them our competition.

▦ Selling Complementary Products and Services

Although our core products are ink and toner cartridges, they are only one component customers need in order to make full use of their printers, copiers, and fax machines. In addition to ink and toner, buyers also need paper, printer cables, and even printer service plans. So as LaserMonks grew, we also grew our product and service offerings in the hopes of earning a larger share of the customer's wallet—we wanted more than ink and toner sales, we also wanted the ancillary product sales. And in adding on those complementary products, we also increased the odds that customers would come back to us for their core need—ink and toner.

Not only did adding such products complete the shopping experience for customers, it also increased revenue and with some product groups, increased our profit margin.

Other companies can create new market space by thinking broadly about the total experience people seek when buying their products or service. What related products do your customers need in order to fully utilize your company's products or services? Are there alliances or joint ventures you should investigate in order to better serve your customers if your company does not have the capabilities internally to meet those needs? The possibilities are almost endless, we discovered.

As we grow, LaserMonks will redefine the scope of the products and service we offer to create an even more complete shopping experience for our customers—and this will mean more than simply product. We will focus less on the pure functionality of the printers and more on the many new and different ways customers can use their printers and computers—for cool projects, improved productivity, and more. This means we will be adding content, such as recommending printers for customers, helping them make printer purchasing decisions, making them aware of new printing technologies, and educating and informing them about new and different ways to use the technology on their desk or in their home.

▣ Looking for an Emotional Appeal

The ink and toner industry has historically competed on rational appeal, that is, on price and performance. Those are the two main criteria customers have been trained to use when selecting both ink and toner products and the retailer(s) they buy from—which has the best price-to-performance ratio.

However, we decided that in order for Laser-Monks to effectively compete in this market, we needed to go beyond the rational argument and build in an emotional appeal. When every other company was relying on rational decision-making, we believed that going a different route would surely make us stand out.

By incorporating an emotional element into each customer interaction with LaserMonks, we have effectively trained customers to expect an emotional reaction. They get used to that good feeling they get from dealing with us and from knowing that in addition to buying a great product, they are also supporting good works. They come away from the buying experience feeling better about themselves and their place in the world, rather than simply feeling satisfied that they can cross off "buy replacement ink cartridges" from their to-do list.

In recent years, the ink and toner industry has really shifted to a commodity market driven by heavy price cutting and an ongoing battle for market share. Although overall growth in the industry has been tremendous, the result of commoditization has been price drops and shrinking margins for ink and toner dealers. To combat this situation, LaserMonks sought to turn a functional product and purchase into a fulfilling and emotional experience.

We do it by selling a concept: "purchasing with a purpose." We reinforce the fact that our proceeds help our communities and we encourage the customer to become involved in this process. At the very least, we try to make them realize that when they make any purchase through LaserMonks they are, in effect, doing good works themselves. This is what allows us to grow and differentiate ourselves from the other Internet retailers and to compete with the national chains.

In addition to trying to differentiate ourselves with our emotional purchase process, we also work to find products without competition—products that will appeal to our customer base and that are not available through other ink and toner outlets. For example, we also sell olive oil, gift baskets, and will soon offer basic consumer products like shampoo, and we provide monk e-cards. Because of our ties to monastic communities, another natural choice for us is products that are made by other monasteries, because the sales of these products helps them support their abbeys.

With these types of monastery-produced products, such as cookies, cakes, and caramels, there is no competition and we can help brother and sister communities sustain themselves with each sale.

Lastly, we have begun to offer "fair trade and socially responsible" products. These are products that empower farmers and artisans around the world to build a better future for themselves, their families, and their communities.

▦ How LaserMonks Fills the Market Space

Although the ink and toner industry was certainly shaped by companies much larger than LaserMonks, we worked to carve out our own niche—creating our own market space—within the industry in a number of ways:

- **Unique Business Model and Message.** No other ink and toner retailer donates its profits to people and organizations in need, as LaserMonks does. Customers feel good about their experience, knowing that their purchase will help others, in addition to receiving the printer supplies they need.

- **Quality Product.** In addition to selling brand name ink and toner cartridges, we also sell very high quality remanufactured and refilled cartridges, for customers who want or need to spend less. We have worked hard to find distributors who provide us with problem-free products and who will stand behind them if problems do occur.

- **Superior Customer Service.** Most companies claim to provide excellent customer service, but we have found that LaserMonks frequently astounds our customers when we demonstrate the lengths to which we are willing to go to satisfy them. Whether it's replacing products and issuing refunds, mailing out totally new printers, or enclosing freebies as a thank-you for their business, we use The Rule of St. Benedict as our model for how our customers—our guests—are to be treated.

- **Competitive Pricing.** Although we do not aim to be the low-cost provider, we do try to keep our prices in line with the majority of other ink and toner retailers. However, we do not participate in pricing wars.

- **Change as the Market Changes.** As a small business, we try to be as responsive as possible to market shifts, whether that means stocking a new product, taking a new approach to inventory management, or redesigning our Web site to meet consumer preferences for information gathering.

- **Creative Approaches to Marketing.** Having started as a cash-poor new business, we learned to be creative in our marketing and promotional efforts out of necessity. Now that we have money to invest in marketing, we still try to make the most of every opportunity.

- **Honesty and Integrity.** Customers, suppliers, and partners know that in every business dealing, we will act with honesty and integrity. They never have to wonder if they will truly receive their order, they know they will. Same goes for whether or not the money actually goes to charity—they know it does.

▨ Using Viral Marketing to Define Our Space

We know that it's not what we say about our products or customer service, or what we say we do with the proceeds, our business and its reputation is what the consumer "experiences" it to be. We can talk about LaserMonks' incredible customer service and hospitality, but if the personal experience of the customer is poor, that is the brand impression that the customer relays to friends, family, and associates.

Understanding this, we work to make sure that every customer experience is a positive one—a very positive one—because we know that in the Internet era, customer experiences are communicated quickly and often to others. That's the power of viral marketing. Conversely, when customers have a bad experience, which we hope they never do at LaserMonks, they are even more apt to tell others about that experience online.

The Internet has made the customer voice more audible and made listening to our customers that much more important. We know that it is easy for people to jump from one Web site to another, which is why we work so hard to keep them at LaserMonks once they arrive. And when they complete their business with us, we want them to spread the word of their purchase and their support of our good works far and wide.

▦ Helping Others Create their Own Market Space

After working through how to define LaserMonks' market space, we branched out to helping other small businesses create their own market space. One of our first clients was a small Midwestern coffee dealer.

While we were in the process of rolling out our Benevolent Blends brand of coffee to our customers, we received a call from the owner of a coffee Web site in need of help to grow his business. He was a long-time importer/exporter and had only recently started the coffee company as a way to spend more time at home with his family.

Since there are plenty of marketing consultants he could turn to for assistance, we asked "Why do you want advice from LaserMonks?" His response was that he is a Catholic who believes in our mission and wants to model his business after ours. He was committed to finding a way to help communities involved in the production of coffee and to sell his product, but he wasn't sure how to go about it, so he turned to us. He had heard about LaserMonks through one of the many newspaper stories that had recently run.

The business was basically a start-up, consisting of a simple Web site the owner had designed himself using Microsoft Word and a small customer base of churches and parishes that purchased the coffee in bulk to sell as fundraisers.

After that initial phone call, we had several more, as well as ongoing e-mail communication, to determine how we could best help him. We wanted to fully understand where the business was and where he wanted to take it, using the LaserMonks business model. Based on those discussions, we mapped out a written strategy and plan for him to follow that looked like this:

- Redesign Web site to enhance content and upgrade functionality and appearance.

- Add shopping cart to enable e-commerce.

- Move site to a new Web hosting service with better service and bandwidth.

- Set up a merchant account so that he could accept credit cards.

- Re-examine fulfillment strategy and consider establishing relationships with drop-shippers.

- Improve site's marketing effectiveness by registering it with search engines.

- Develop an e-mail marketing strategy for his current customer base.

- Work on further developing his unique selling proposition (USP), which was selling to religious institutions for fundraising, such as by private labeling.

- Identify other complementary products his market might be attracted to, such as hot cocoa and T-shirts.

- Lower his cost structure to increase his profit margin.

- Improve how the Web site communicates his business model of donating part of the proceeds to good works worldwide.

Although many of these concepts were second-nature to us, having tackled them as we built Laser-Monks, it became obvious that some were very new to him. For example, the issue of how a company evaluates the benefits, both in cost and quality, of drop-shipping versus handling shipping in-house was new territory.

We had many conversations about his shipping model as we led him through the maze of questions he needed to ask and answer. There were questions of accuracy and speed of delivery, of filling orders with different products, and of the impact on delivery cost if one vendor was also responsible for packing ancillary products. How to negotiate with the vendor regarding handling fees per order, how to ensure the vendor is an accurate shipper, and how to handle the daily billing cost of the drop-shipped orders, these issues we tackled one-by-one, as well as the challenge of accurately tracking and monitoring total costs and payments.

Together we developed a fulfillment solution that fit his business well. We also spent a good deal of time discussing his current customer demographic and whether he wanted to branch out to reach other markets.

There isn't a magic wand that anyone can wave, including us, that will move a company from five orders a day to 400 overnight. Creating and defining the market space for LaserMonks has been many parts hard work, many parts creativity and the openness to look at tasks from the outside in, many parts good, solid business practices, and the blessing of media attention when we were ready for it.

Our mission now is to assist other businesses in increasing their market share and, at the same time, to encourage them to consider a business model that involves designating a portion of their increased proceeds to good works.

We are also focusing on educating religious and nonprofit groups in creating for-profit businesses to fund their nonprofit missions.

That is how we've carved out our market space, and we believe it's a strategy that can work for virtually any kind of business. We hope that it works for yours.

resources

Many thanks and blessings to our various partners: Benedictine Sisters of Mount Angel, Benedictine Sisters of Perpetual Adoration, Brighton USA, Busted Halo, Chris Eden, Cistercian Publications, Evans Printing, exacttarget.com, Gotvmail, The Greenery, Sparta, WI, Happy Dog Yards, LLC., Identity Works, Michael Johnson, Mission Farm Bakery, Nick the Roaster, Olsten Staffing, Our Lady of the Mississippi Abbey, Pack Plus Converting, Redwoods Monastery, St. Joseph's Abbey, San Benito Monastery, Dayton, WY, Sisters of St. Benedict, Sisters of the Holy Spirit, U.S. Postal Service–Sparta Branch, Volusion, Inc., Zencart Ecommerce.

index